Why Do You Need This New Edition?

If you're wondering why you should buy this new edition of PSYCHOBABBLE AND BIOBUNK: Using Psychological Science to Think Critically About Popular Psychology, here are 21 good reasons!

This third edition of *Psychobabble and Biobunk* contains twenty completely new essays and book reviews. The review of *The Nurture Assumption* has been retained from the previous edition to round out the "Personality, Motivation, and Development" section. The essays and book reviews presented here are:

Thinking Critically—and Why We Often Don't

1. *"Why Won't They Admit They're Wrong?" and Other Skeptics' Mysteries*, by Carol Tavris and Elliot Aronson

Personality, Motivation, and Development

2. *Outliers: The story of success*, by Malcolm Gladwell
3. *Men to Boys: The making of modern immaturity*, by Gary Cross
4. *Understanding Attachment: Parenting, child care, and emotional development*, by Jean Mercer
5. *Love at Goon Park: Harry Harlow and the science of affection*, by Deborah Blum
6. *Happiness: Lessons from a new science*, by Richard Layard
   Making Happy People: The nature of happiness and its origins in childhood, by Paul Martin
   Going Sane, by Adam Phillips
7. *Bright-Sided: How the relentless promotion of positive thinking has undermined America*, by Barbara Ehrenreich
8. *The Nurture Assumption: Why children turn out the way they do*, by Judith Rich Harris
9. *Personality: What makes you the way you are*, by Daniel Nettle
10. *"Are Girls As Mean As They Say They Are?"* (review essay)

Psychotherapy and the Scientist-Practitioner Gap

11. *The Body Never Lies: The lingering effects of hurtful parenting*, by Alice Miller
12. *Into the Minds of Madmen: How the FBI's behavioral science unit revolutionized crime investigation*, by Don DeNevi and John H. Campbell
13. *Remembering Trauma*, by Richard J. McNally
    Out of the Dark, by Linda Caine and Robin Royston
14. *In Therapy We Trust: America's obsession with self-fulfillment*, by Eva S. Moskowitz
15. *Prisoners of Hate: The cognitive basis of anger, hostility, and violence*, by Aaron T. Beck
16. *Making Us Crazy: DSM: The psychiatric bible and the creation of mental disorders*, by Herb Kutchins and Stuart A. Kirk
17. *Of Two Minds: The growing disorder in American psychiatry*, by T. M. Luhrmann

Research Methods and Social Issues

18. *The Hungry Gene: The science of fat and the future of thin*, by Ellen Ruppel Shell
19. *The Genius Factory: Unravelling the mysteries of the Nobel Prize sperm bank*, by David Plotz
20. *Rape: A history from 1860 to the present*, by Joanna Bourke
21. *Sex and the Psyche*, by Brett Kahr

PSYCHOBABBLE AND BIOBUNK

USING PSYCHOLOGICAL SCIENCE TO THINK CRITICALLY ABOUT POPULAR PSYCHOLOGY

Third Edition

Carol Tavris

Prentice Hall

Boston   Columbus   Indianapolis   New York   San Francisco
Upper Saddle River   Amsterdam   Cape Town   Dubai   London   Madrid
Milan   Munich   Paris   Montreal   Toronto   Delhi   Mexico City   Sao Paulo
Sydney   Hong Kong   Seoul   Singapore   Taipei   Tokyo

11/26/12
Gbg
$26.40

Editor in Chief: Jessica Mosher
Executive Editor: Stephen Frail
Managing Editor, Editorial: Judy Casillo
Director Of Marketing: Brandy Dawson
Senior Marketing Manager:
  Laura Lee Manley
Managing Editor: Maureen Richardson
Project Manager: Renata Butera
Operations Specialist: Renata Butera

Creative Art Director: Jayne Conte
Cover Designer: Bruce Kenselaar
Cover Credit: Flame © Anton Bryksin
Full-Service Project Management:
  Mohinder Singh / Aptara®, Inc.
Composition: Aptara®, Inc.
Printer/Binder: Courier Stoughton
Cover Printer: Courier Stoughton
Text Font: Times 10/12

Except where otherwise noted, the reviews in this book appeared, in an earlier form, in the *Times Literary Supplement* between 1999 and 2010. Reprinted with permission from the TLS.
Essay 1 Reprinted with permission from *Skeptical Inquirer,* November/December 2007, by Carol Tavris and Elliot Aronson.
Essay 5 Reprinted with permission from *American Scientist,* March/April 2003.
Essay 8 Reprinted with permission from the *New York Times Book Review,* September 13, 1998.
Essay 10 Reprinted with permission from the *Chronicle of Higher Education,* July 5, 2002.

Library of Congress Cataloging-in-Publication Data
Tavris, Carol.
  Psychobabble and biobunk: using psychological science to think critically about popular psychology / Carol Tavris.—3rd ed.
    p. cm.
  Rev. ed. of: Psychobabble & biobunk: using psychology to think critically about issues in the news : opinion essays and book reviews. 2nd ed. 2001.
  Includes bibliographical references and index.
  ISBN-13: 978-0-205-01591-7 (alk. paper)
  ISBN-10: 0-205-01591-3 (alk. paper)
1. Psychology. 2. Social psychology. 3. Psychotherapy.
I. Tavris, Carol. Psychobabble & biobunk. II. Title.
  BF121.T327 2011
  150—dc22

                                                    2010038015

10 9 8 7 6 5 4 3 2 1

Prentice Hall
is an imprint of

www.pearsonhighered.com

ISBN 10:   0-205-01591-3
ISBN 13: 978-0-205-01591-7

Contents

PSYCHOTHERAPY AND THE SCIENTIST-PRACTITIONER GAP

RESEARCH METHODS AND SOCIAL ISSUES

A Note to the Reader

The essays and book reviews collected here were written primarily for the *TLS (Times Literary Supplement)*, with a few others for *The Chronicle of Higher Education, Skeptical Inquirer,* and *The New York Times Book Review.* My goal has long been to show how psychological research can help people assess all sorts of matters discussed in the popular culture and promoted by best-selling books (and others that would like to be). I hope these articles will provide a springboard for your own evaluation and analysis of these issues.

In our introductory psychology textbooks *Psychology* and *Invitation to Psychology,* Carole Wade and I define "critical thinking" as the ability and willingness to assess claims and make judgments on the basis of well-supported reasons. Feelings aren't enough, personal experience and anecdotes aren't enough, and shouting down the opposition isn't enough. We identify eight guidelines for critical and creative thinking, which we hope readers will find useful in thinking about the issues raised by the articles in this collection:

➤ *Ask questions; be willing to wonder.* To think critically you must be willing to think creatively—to be curious about the puzzles of human behavior, to wonder why people act the way they do, and to question received wisdom and examine new explanations of why things are as they are. (See Essay 10, a review of a spate of books on adolescent girls.)

➤ *Define your terms.* Identify the problem in clear and concrete terms, rather than vague ones like "happiness," "potential," or "self-esteem." (See Essay 3, on Gary Cross's efforts to define maturity, and Essays 6 and 7, reviews of books on ways of defining and measuring happiness.)

➤ *Examine the evidence.* Consider the nature of the evidence supporting various approaches to the problem under examination. *Is* there good evidence, one way or another? Is it reliable? Valid? Is the "evidence" merely someone's personal assertion or speculation, or is it based on replicated empirical data? (See Essay 13, a review of Richard J. McNally's *Remembering Trauma,* a sterling assessment of the empirical evidence regarding trauma and memory, contrasted with a pop-psych book whose claims are completely unsupported.)

➤ *Analyze assumptions and biases—your own and those of others.* What prejudices, deeply held values, and other biases do you bring to your evaluation of a problem? Are you willing to consider evidence that contradicts your beliefs? Can you identify the assumptions and biases that others bring to their arguments? (See Essays 8 and 9, reviews of Judith Rich Harris's controversial book *The Nurture Assumption* and Daniel Nettle's *Personality,* which question the widely held assumption that parents have the most powerful effect on their children's personality and behavior throughout life.)

➤ *Avoid emotional reasoning.* The fact that you feel strongly about something doesn't make you right! Everyone holds convictions about how the world operates (or how it should), and other people are probably as serious about their convictions as you are about yours. Feelings are important, but they should not substitute for careful appraisal of arguments and evidence. (See Essay 11, a review of Alice Miller's notion that "the body never lies," and Essay 20, a review of Joanna Bourke's history of rape.)

➤ *Don't oversimplify.* Look beyond the obvious; reject simplistic thinking ("All the evil in the world is due to that group of loathsome people") and either-or thinking ("Either genes determine everything about personality and behavior or they count for virtually nothing"). Be wary of "argument by anecdote," taking a single case as evidence of a larger phenomenon. (See Essay 12, a review of a book on the oversimplifications and distortions that often accompany efforts at criminal profiling.)

➤ *Consider other interpretations.* Before you draw a conclusion from the evidence, think creatively about other possible explanations. When you learn that two events are statistically correlated, for example, be sure to think carefully about which one is the cause and which the result—or whether a third factor might be causing both of them. (See Essay 2, a review of Malcolm Gladwell's hugely popular *Outliers,* which unfortunately cherry-picks the data to present only one side of a complex argument.)

➤ *Tolerate uncertainty.* This is probably the hardest step in becoming a critical thinker, for it requires that we hold our beliefs lightly enough that we can give them up when better evidence comes along. It requires us to live with the realization that we may not have the perfect answer to a problem at the moment, and may never have it. Many people want "the" answers, and they want science to provide them: "Just tell me what to do!" they demand. Pseudoscience promises answers, which is why it is so popular; science gives us probabilities that suggest that one answer is better than another—for now—and warns us that one day we may have to change our minds. (See Essay 1, on how the mechanism of cognitive dissonance and self-justification makes it difficult for all of us to tolerate uncertainty; why, once we take a position on an issue or belief, it becomes more difficult to change our minds—let alone admit we were wrong.)

There are many ways to use this collection of essays in the classroom—not only in courses in psychology but also in sociology, speech, political science, English composition, and other disciplines. Some instructors may assign the articles as supplementary readings. Others may decide to use them to stimulate class discussions, or assign them as topics for written assignments and exercises. Students can be asked to say why they agree or disagree with the arguments expressed in a given essay, to cite evidence to support their argument, or to identify the critical thinking guidelines that are most salient in it. They may be asked to think of further questions they would want to raise after reading an article.

Carole and I realize that these guidelines are not the only ones possible. They do not include all skills of logic and debate, every principle of scientific reasoning, nor all the mental and emotional obstacles to critical thinking. But they do capture the core elements of scientific and independent thinking. Using them, you will undoubtedly be able to discover my own lapses of critical thinking! I hope that these essays will interest you, amuse you, and, most of all, sharpen your own thoughts about the issues they raise.

—Carol Tavris

About the Author

Carol Tavris earned her Ph.D. in the interdisciplinary program in social psychology at the University of Michigan, and as a writer and lecturer she has sought to educate the public about the importance of critical and scientific thinking in psychology. Her textbooks with Carole Wade include *Psychology; Invitation to Psychology; Psychology in Perspective;* and *The Longest War: Sex differences in perspective.* Dr. Tavris is also coauthor, with Elliot Aronson, of *Mistakes Were Made (But Not by Me): Why we justify foolish beliefs, bad decisions, and hurtful acts;* and author of *The Mismeasure of Woman* and *Anger: The misunderstood emotion.* She has written on psychological topics for a wide variety of magazines, journals, edited books, and newspapers. (Twenty-one of her book reviews and opinion essays for the TLS and other publications have been collected in this reader, *Psychobabble and Biobunk.*) Dr. Tavris lectures widely on topics involving science vs. pseudoscience in psychology and psychiatry, on writing about science for the public, and many other subjects of contemporary interest. She has taught in the psychology department at UCLA and at the Human Relations Center of the New School for Social Research in New York. She is a Fellow of the American Psychological Association and a charter Fellow of the Association for Psychological Science; a fellow of the Center for Inquiry; and a member of the editorial board of the APS journal *Psychological Science in the Public Interest.*

PART I

THINKING CRITICALLY—AND WHY WE OFTEN DON'T

1

■ ■ ■

"Why Won't They Admit They're Wrong?" and Other Skeptics' Mysteries

By Carol Tavris and Elliot Aronson

One of the greatest challenges for scientists and educators is how to persuade people to give up beliefs they hold dear when the evidence clearly indicates that they should. Why aren't most people grateful for the data? It's easy to make fun of others who won't give up ideas or practices that scientific research has shown to be demonstrably wrong—therapeutic touch, alien abduction, the Rorschach Inkblot Test—or beliefs in haunted houses and psychic detective skills that *The Skeptical Inquirer* keeps exposing as frauds or delusions. It's harder to see that the mechanism that keeps all these people from admitting they are wrong afflicts us too—all of us, even skeptics.

The motivational mechanism that underlies the reluctance to be wrong, to change our minds, to admit serious mistakes, and to be unwilling to accept unwelcome findings is cognitive dissonance. The theory of cognitive dissonance was invented fifty years ago by Leon Festinger, who defined "dissonance" as a state of tension that occurs whenever a person holds two cognitions that are psychologically inconsistent, such as "Smoking is a dumb thing to do because it could kill me" and "I smoke two packs a day." Dissonance produces mental discomfort, a state that is as unpleasant as extreme hunger, and people don't rest easy until they find a way to reduce it. Smokers can reduce dissonance either by quitting or

Skeptical Inquirer, November/December 2007.

by convincing themselves that smoking isn't really so harmful. Hey, in fact, it's beneficial, since it keeps me from gaining weight. The Congressmen and ministers who preach that homosexuality is a sin and a choice reduce dissonance, when caught with male lovers, by saying, "I'm not gay—I was just under stress."

In a sense, dissonance theory is a theory of our mental blind spots, of how and why we block information that might make us question our behavior or convictions. The theory has been supported by many discoveries in cognitive science that have identified the built-in biases of the human mind. One of the most effective ways the mind has of keeping our beliefs consonant, for example, is through the confirmation bias: the fact that we notice and remember information that confirms what we believe, and ignore or forget information that disconfirms it. (Indeed, one of the reasons that scientific thinking does not come naturally to many people is precisely because it requires the investigator to consider disconfirming—dissonant—evidence for a hypothesis.) Another central bias is the belief that *we* aren't biased; everyone else is. *We* see things clearly; what is the matter with those people? What are they *thinking?* What they are thinking, of course, is that they see things clearly and we don't.

Dissonance is uncomfortable enough when two cognitions conflict, but it is most painful when an important element of the self-concept is threatened, for example, when information disputes how we see ourselves, challenges a central religious, political, or intellectual belief, or questions a memory or a story we use to explain our lives. When that happens, the easiest way to reduce dissonance is simply to reject the information (it's stupid, it's flat-out wrong) or kill the messenger (he's biased, after all). But even more significantly, when people behave in a way that is inconsistent with their own view of themselves as good, smart, ethical, and kind, they will tend to reduce dissonance not by changing those self-concepts but by justifying their behavior to themselves. If I am good and kind, then by definition the bad or unkind thing I did was warranted: *They started it. He deserved it. Everyone does it. I was only following orders.*

The nonconscious mechanism of self-justification is not the same thing as lying or making excuses to others to save face or save a job. It is more powerful and more dangerous than the explicit lie, because it blinds us from even becoming aware that we are wrong about a belief or that we did something foolish, unethical, or cruel. Dissonance theory, therefore, predicts that it's not only bad people who do bad things. More often, the greater problem comes from good people who do bad things or smart people who cling to foolish beliefs, precisely to preserve their belief that they are good, smart people.

This is why, when skeptics wave their reams of data at people who have just sold their house and cow to follow a delusional prophet of Doomsday, what they are mostly doing is making the followers feel stupid. How much more soothing it is for the followers to justify their actions by saying, "Thank God, we sold the house and cow for our brilliant leader! Our devotion

4

spared the world from disaster." This was precisely the reasoning of the followers of a Doomsday prophet whom Festinger and his colleagues described in their great early study of dissonance in action, *When Prophecy Fails.*

Scientists as well as pseudoscientists fall prey to self-justification. Most scientists pride themselves on their intellectual integrity, yet, with the breakdown of the former firewall between research and commerce, their intellectual independence is being whittled away. Many scientists, like plants turning toward the sun, are turning toward the interests of their sponsors without even being aware that they are doing so. When investigators have compared the results of studies funded independently and those funded by industry, they have consistently uncovered a "funding bias." In a typical example, 161 studies, all published during the same six-year span, examined the possible risks to human health of four chemicals. Of the studies funded by industry, only 14 percent found harmful effects on health; of those funded independently, fully 60 percent found harmful effects.

Most of the scientists funded by industry are not consciously cheating, nor are they corrupt, like the few who blatantly fake data to win fame and fortune. Rather, they are decent people who have the same cognitive blind spots we all do. If you are an independent scientist and your research turns up an ambiguous finding about your new drug—perhaps a slightly increased risk of heart attack—you will probably say, "This is troubling; let's investigate further. Is this increased risk a fluke, was it due to the drug, or were the patients unusually vulnerable?" However, if you are motivated to show that your new drug is effective and better than older drugs, you will unwittingly lean in the direction of resolving the ambiguity in your sponsor's favor. "It was a fluke. Those patients were already quite sick, anyway." This was the reasoning of the Merck-funded investigators who had been studying the company's multibillion-dollar drug Vioxx before evidence of the drug's risks was produced by independent scientists. In the need to reduce dissonance, the Merck-funded scientists are no different from people who believe in the efficacy of the Rorschach or therapeutic touch. By justifying their decision to support the drug and minimize disconfirming data, they preserve their feelings of integrity and of being above the conflicts of interest that so clearly taint everyone else's judgments.

Cognitive dissonance is hard wired, but how we choose to reduce it is not. Just as good drivers learn to correct for that blind spot in their rear vision, good thinkers can learn to correct for the blind spots in their reasoning. No, in *our* reasoning. Scientists must be just as vigilant about biases and conflicts of interest that can affect their work as they are about biases in others' research. And we can all try to avoid that tone of "we think skeptically and you don't." One exercise in humility is to recall the dissonant pangs of embarrassment we felt when we, too, shut our own minds to evidence to preserve a cherished belief. Our colleagues and loved ones will thank us for admitting it. And who knows? We might actually learn a little something from the mistakes we made.

5

PART II

PERSONALITY, MOTIVATION, AND DEVELOPMENT

2

■ ■ ■

Outliers

The Story of Success

By Malcolm Gladwell

Do people who rise to the top of their professions do so because of sheer native talent, persistence, ambition, creativity, and perhaps a dollop of narcissism and obsessiveness? If you think so, argues Malcolm Gladwell in *Outliers,* you are mistaken. Success has little or nothing to do with personality, genius, or drive; it results from the interaction of a person's immediate circumstances, cultural legacy, economic and educational opportunities, and random bolts of luck. "This is not a book about tall trees," he writes. "It's a book about forests."

Gladwell retells the familiar "story of success," the one in which hard work and go-it-alone determination are rewarded with riches and fulfillment, the one whose moral is "anyone can become anything if they try hard enough." He does so in his usual style, with immense charm and clarity, weaving persuasive anecdotes with carefully selected studies to support his points. "No one—not rock stars, not professional athletes, not software billionaires, and not even geniuses—ever makes it alone," he writes. Superstars in any field "are products of history and community, of opportunity and legacy. Their success is not exceptional or mysterious. It is grounded in a web of advantages and inheritances, some deserved, some not, some earned, some just plain lucky—but all critical to making them who they are. The outlier, in the end, is not an outlier at all."

Well, yes and no. Gladwell's easy-going style blurs the important distinction between outliers and other successful people. Outliers are, by definition, the statistical rarities who fall at the furthest end of the bell curve. Gladwell uses the word, however, to refer not only to supremely gifted individuals but also to groups of people who simply succeeded beyond expectation when their circumstances changed, such as the black children fortunate to be admitted to the more than 50 KIPP schools across the U.S. (KIPP stands for "Knowledge Is Power Program.") Unlike their inner-city peers trapped in miserable schools and economically depressed communities, more than 80 per cent of KIPP graduates go on to college. They are the beneficiaries of being in a particular kind of school, one that demands and rewards constant study, hard work, and persistence, but these children are not outliers in the same sense that Bill Gates and the Beatles are. A KIPP school, however, will certainly increase the chances that any potential outliers among them will emerge.

"Because we so profoundly personalize success," Gladwell writes, "we miss opportunities to lift others onto the top rung." It would be more accurate to say that we miss opportunities to lift others *onto the ladder.* But just as Gladwell blurs the meaning of outlier, he blurs the meanings of success: Sometimes it refers to geniuses and superstars; sometimes to average Chinese children whose language gives them a head start in math; sometimes to Korean pilots who learn to overcome a cultural legacy of deference to authority so they can stand up to their tired superior officers and avoid crashing planes; sometimes to people like his Jamaican mother, who benefitted from events in Jamaican history that gave her a chance for higher education. "Extraordinary achievement is less about talent than it is about opportunity," says Gladwell, while adding that of course a basic minimum of talent and intelligence is required. In fact, his book shows that a basic minimum of *ordinary* achievement is less about talent and intelligence than about opportunity, but then he would have had to jettison that flattering, provocative word, outlier.

Likewise, in his discussion of the role of chance events, Gladwell fails to ask why some people are able to take advantage of their lucky breaks, whereas others in the same circumstances do not. If Bill Joy had not happened to be at the University of Michigan in 1971 and thus been able to make use of the university's free, unlimited computer access (unavailable almost anywhere else at the time), he would never have ended up co-founding Sun Microsystems and making a fortune in computers. True, but how many of the Michigan students who used its free computer became Bill Joy? Only one. If the Mothers' Club of Lakeside Academy had not bought Bill Gates a computer in 1968, Bill Gates might have … what? Gone into the biscuit business? How do we know whether or not he would have accomplished just as much by another route? That is the problem with arguing by anecdote, even the terrific anecdotes that Gladwell chooses. How many people given the *same* opportunities become leaders in their field, great artists, prescient executives, or innovative scientists?

Gladwell has often been criticized for taking a concept and selecting stories and data to fit, a method of book-writing that creates what some skeptics call the "except when it doesn't" problem: The premise of *Blink* is that your first intuitive guess is likely to be right, except when it is wrong.

The premise of *The Tipping Point* is that a series of small events can become a tipping point for society-wide change, except when they don't. And the premise of *Outliers* is that extraordinary success depends on culture, circumstances, demographics, and chance, except when it also depends on talent, willingness to break rules, imagination, and risk-taking. Success depends on being in the right place at the right time, except for all those other people who were in the same place at the same time and didn't even notice that the time was right.

Nonetheless, the studies and examples that Gladwell assembles are pearls. Even if he does not string them together to make a necklace, they will, taken singly, delight and surprise his readers. To illustrate the power of "utterly arbitrary advantage," for example, he describes the way that hockey-mad Canadians select 9- and 10-year-old boys for the traveling all-star teams, consisting of players who seem to have the greatest promise of success in the sport. If you are a boy born in the first few months of the year, you are far more likely to be bigger and stronger than boys born at the end of the year. Thus, in selecting among 10-year-olds who show the most promise in hockey, Canadians start with a false definition of who the best 10-year-old players are—the oldest ones. These boys then get better coaching and more practice, and within a few years they *are* the best players. The same selection process occurs in kindergarten and first grade, where teachers often confuse maturity with ability. The more mature children get more attention, are more likely to be put into gifted classes, and are otherwise given more educational benefits; before long they *are* the best students. Initial small differences may not matter much at the beginning, but over time, they accumulate into larger, more significant advantages.

Gladwell also debunks the popular belief that some people just have what it takes, naturally, to achieve. "There are no 'naturals,' who get to the top no matter how little they practice," he writes, "and no 'grinds,' who practice massively and don't make it." He contends that the single most important difference between the amateur and the pro, between the good and the brilliant, between the failure and the star, is sheer hours of practice, and 10,000 hours is the "magic number of greatness." The Beatles, starting off as unknowns in Hamburg, played 8 hours straight, 7 nights a week; Bill Gates, having discovered computers, became obsessed with them, working on them morning and night, every day of the week.

Gladwell is to be commended for emphasizing the importance of practice and persistence, especially when so many American children think that if first you don't succeed, you're "stupid." Yet, again, readers may wonder about the thousands of computer geeks who spend countless hours at the keyboard without becoming much of anything, or the legions of boys who spend thousands of hours on the basketball court and do not become Michael Jordan. (They get damned good, though.) Moreover, we may ask what it is about high achievers that makes them *want* to spend ten thousand hours

11

practicing the piccolo or doing whatever else they love, a question that surely invites an answer or two from the tallest trees in the forest.

Gladwell makes a bit of fun of Jeb Bush, son of one former president and brother of another, for saying that "overall, it's a disadvantage" being a president's son, and that he got where he was solely by working "real hard." The Bush family's blindness to the benefits of privilege is pretty funny, but it should not blind us, or Gladwell, to the many sons and daughters of privilege who, unable to take advantage of their lucky breaks, achieve nothing. Outliers, after all, lie on both ends of the bell curve.

3

■ ■ ■

Men to Boys
The Making of Modern Immaturity

By Gary Cross

W hat is maturity? Gary Cross, a historian of American popular culture, never defines it, but he knows what it isn't. Everywhere he turns, he sees "men who refuse to grow up—husbands of 35 who enjoy playing the same video games that obsess 12-year-olds; boyfriends who will not commit to marriage or family; and fathers who fight with umpires or coaches at their son's little league games. We all know men in their thirties or forties who would rather tinker with their cars than interact with their families, fathers who want to share in their children's fads, and even bosses and political leaders who act like impulsive teenagers. Many are frustrated and confused about what maturity is and whether they can or want to achieve it. I call them boy-men."

Certainly we are all familiar with the childish males of many contemporary films and novels, the scruffy Peter Pans who just want to play and party, uninterested in any requirements of love or work that might deflect them from their immediate pleasures. Some are young men who don't want to grow up, and others are grown men trying to be young.

Cross is not concerned with the women who try to dress and talk like their teenage daughters, "want to share in their children's fads," fight with coaches at their daughter's games, or are obsessed with youth and fears of aging. This omission would have been fine if Cross's goal was to explore the changing meanings of manhood in a time when serving in the military and being a family's sole provider are no longer the key markers.

Times Literary Supplement, October 10, 2008.

But for a book about "the making of modern immaturity," Cross needs to explain what differentiates boy-men from girl-women in a gender-blind marketing of products that promise perpetual youth and an economy based on excessive consumption. The invisibility of women as a comparison group weakens his case: "Most men of my father's generation did not become Beats, playboys, or hot-rodders," he writes, "but many found wish fulfillment in reading *On the Road,* the 'Playboy Advisor,' or *Hot Rod Magazine.* This was part of a silent revolt from providership." Revolt? Why not a momentary escape from providership, just as watching "Sex and the City" or reading advice columns and *People* might be for women?

The challenge of Cross's fascinating subject is not only to identify issues that are particular to men rather than women, but also to separate what is truly different in contemporary culture from psychology-as-usual in different guise. Elders in every generation love to complain about the ignorance and foolishness of the young and their new-fangled inventions that are sure to destroy society. (Sumerian parents probably complained about the invention of the wheel: "Humans have done just fine without it for 143,000 years, and now the kids will never do any work!") Although Cross is aware of this trap, he falls into it frequently, as in his assessment of video games. At least he doesn't blame them for making their young players violent, though he cannot resist mentioning the irrelevant fact that some American teenagers who went on rampage killings were avid players. In fact, rates of adolescent violence have been plummeting in the decades that video game popularity soared.

No, Cross's complaint about video games is that they contribute to the prolonged immaturity of males: "Video games induce otherwise 'mature' men to forgo relationships with women and family... for the highly individualistic and largely isolated encounter with the ephemeral thrill." And in the era before video games, did "mature" men have deep relationships with women and family or did they prefer poker, sports, bars, and building sailboats in the basement? "These games," he adds, "reinforce the childish view that the world is full of bogeymen under the bed and the equally childish response, the cathartic thrill of zapping them." A childish view indeed, but unfortunately one that describes people of all ages, starting with how adults have always regarded the enemy. What, pray, were grown-up Americans of the 1950s doing during the Cold War but reinforcing the childish view that world was full of Communist bogeymen in movies and schools? Does Cross think that most adult citizens do not feel a cathartic thrill of "zapping" the enemy during wartime? How about at a soccer game?

As a cultural historian, Cross focuses on the culture-wide "rejection of maturity" through the lens of changes in television, film, cultural heroes, clothes, and the panoply of entertainments from Disneyland to video games. The resulting romp is great fun for charter members of the baby-boom generation, who get to feel nostalgic about the past and justified in their complaints about contemporary culture, but it's not a satisfying explanation of anything. Many of the book's pronouncements disintegrate like dandelions if you breathe on them. Thus one of Cross's implicit notions of maturity is that "to grow up [once] meant abandoning fantasy and mere thrills for cultivated and complex pleasures." It did? Cultivated and complex pleasures are nice for those who have time, education, and money for the opera, *Ulysses*, and polo; but abandoning fantasy? All human beings have fantasies, whether internally generated in daydreams or vicariously indulged in books and films from *Beowulf* to *Batman*. Fantasies are the escape clauses in our life sentences.

Nonetheless, Cross is on to an interesting phenomenon: There is something different about the idea of maturity today. The word itself sounds old-fashioned, a word used by some authoritarian elder who regards having fun as a threat to the social order. (Cross feels obliged to defend fun, though he adds that "Sometimes it is hard to tell the difference between fun-loving men and boy-men." I'll say.) Once it was easy to know when you were an adult: The milestones of life told you. You got an adult job and grown-up clothes; you had your first sexual affair; if you were a man, you served in the military; you outgrew your "puppy" loves and got married; and you became a parent in your early twenties.

The sweeping demographic and economic changes following the Second World War, however, threw these timelines out of whack for millions of people, leading to the postponement of career decisions, marriage or cohabitation, and parenthood until, on average, a person's late twenties or thirties. Globalization changed the world of work and the reliability of jobs; children of baby-boomers have fewer opportunities and much less lifetime career security than their parents.

So widespread are these changes that developmental psychologists now speak of a phase of life between adolescence and adulthood, "emerging adulthood," roughly between ages eighteen and twenty-five. Young people in this category are usually in college or professional schools, or in low-paying temporary jobs, and therefore, at least partly dependent financially on their parents—the biggest cause of their "immaturity." They are the group most likely to live unstable lives, feel unrooted, and take risks. Emerging adults move more often than other demographic groups do—back to their parents' homes and then out again, from one city to another, from living with roommates to living on their own. They don't put down roots, as their parents did at their age, and their rates of risky behavior (such as binge drinking, having unprotected sex, and driving at high speeds or while drunk) are higher than those of any other age group, including adolescents.

Cross acknowledges these demographic and economic changes, but he does not make them the centerpiece of his analysis, and the result feels like a book about icing rather than cake. If jobs are not available, why not experiment with different ones? If jobs are not secure, why not scale back your ambitions? If the career trajectory is no longer secure from first hiring to retirement, why not try another field? If marriages seem so likely to break up, what is the hurry to enter one? And if everything is relative, the world can't be saved, and nothing is true, why sacrifice now for tomorrow when you could be out having fun?

Cross attributes the demise of maturity in behavior, dress, humor, culture, and values, and the corresponding rise of a culture devoted to endless thrills, to the baby-boom generation's rejection of the Victorian, patriarchal model of fatherhood and deference to authority, the rise of feminism, and technological innovation. These developments were not entirely bad, he agrees; feminism allowed men to become better, more involved fathers—at least those men eventually willing to take on fatherhood. But, he argues, these changes also "reduced the 'payoff' of patriarchy and its culture of restraint, refinement, and responsibility. These changes both emasculated men ... and also reduced male responsibility in work and family, making their lives less 'mature'." Without an intelligent standard of maturity to replace the dated Victorian model, the market did it for us, selling the values of self-indulgence, consumption, and thrills. As youth culture was commercialized and institutionalized, its attitudes came to dominate across generations, including its puerile, bathroom humor, cynicism to-ward relationships, and attraction to "displays of aestheticized violence."

I understand what Cross is complaining about, but I wish he had paid less attention to television shows and spent some time examining the meanings of maturity in today's world. In the absence of external markers set by marriage, parenthood, and career advancement, what does it mean to be a grown-up? Chronology no longer confers an answer: Some 15-year-olds are more mature than some 45-year-olds who dress, think and act like 15-year-olds.

Today's markers of maturity are internal qualities; for me, the list would include coming to terms with roads not taken, accepting disappointments, not blaming one's parents for everything wrong in one's life, taking responsibility for decisions that went awry, having guiding beliefs and living by them, stepping up to the plate when it comes time to care for loved ones who are ill or in trouble, and having commitments to people and causes larger than oneself. Maturity is not like scurvy, something people do or do not "have." It is something we achieve, through experience, work, trial and error, love and loss. We can be grown up in some domains and childish in others. We can achieve some measure of it early, when we have to, or delay it for decades. We can strive to attain it or have it forced upon us by events.

"Freedom," wrote Jean-Paul Sartre, "is what you do with what has been done to you." So is maturity.

4

■ ■ ■

Understanding Attachment
Parenting, Child Care, and Emotional Development

By Jean Mercer

"Attachment" is a growing industry in psychology. People long for it, are biologically wired for it, depend on it, and then, taking it for granted, kick it around all too casually.

Only in America could a phenomenon that is as natural as breathing be turned into a commodity, with products, toys, techniques, and therapies alleged to help parents bond to their children and vice versa. Every so often, one of these therapies goes tragically awry, and the assumptions underlying its practice reach public awareness. In May 2000, in Colorado, the police arrested four people on charges of recklessly causing the death of 10-year-old Candace Newmaker during a session of "rebirthing" therapy.

In the procedure, which its proponents claim helps adopted children form attachments to their adoptive parents by reliving their birth, the child was completely wrapped in a blanket and surrounded by large pillows. The therapists then pressed in on the pillows to simulate contractions and told the girl to push her way out of the blanket over her head.

Candace repeatedly said that she could not breathe and felt she was going to die. But instead of unwrapping her, the therapists said, "You've got to push hard if you want to be born—or do you want to stay in there and die?" Candace lost consciousness and was rushed to a local hospital, where she died the next day. Connell Watkins and Julie Ponder, unlicensed

Times Literary Supplement, October 6, 2006.

social workers who operated the counseling center, were sentenced to 16 years in prison for reckless child abuse resulting in death. Tragically, Candace was not the only victim. Dozens of other children have died during this kind of therapy.

Rebirthing therapy is one of a variety of punitive practices, collectively referred to as "Attachment Therapy," that allegedly help adopted and foster children bond with their new parents. These techniques include withholding food, isolating the children for extended periods, humiliating them, and requiring them to spend hours sitting motionless. (Proponents of these tactics apparently confuse a child's exhausted, terrified capitulation with bonding.) The American Psychiatric Association officially opposes attachment therapies, noting that "there is *no* scientific evidence to support the effectiveness of such interventions," and so has the American Professional Society on the Abuse of Children.

Attachment is indisputably central to children's development, as the psychiatrist John Bowlby showed in the aftermath of World War II. Bowlby had observed the devastating effects on babies raised in orphanages without touches or cuddles: They were physically healthy, but emotionally despairing, remote, and listless. Emotional attachment, said Bowlby, gives a baby a sustenance as crucial as food. By becoming attached to their caregivers, children gain a secure base from which they can explore the environment and a haven of safety to return to when they are afraid. Attachment is the lifespring of trust and love.

The next question was: Is attachment a unitary thing or does it come in different varieties? Mary Ainsworth, who had worked with Bowlby in London in the 1950s, wanted to measure attachment, not just describe it, and in the 1960s she devised an experimental method of measurement called the Strange Situation. A mother brings her baby into an unfamiliar room containing lots of toys. After a while, a stranger comes in and attempts to play with the child. The mother leaves the baby with the stranger. She then returns and plays with the child, and the stranger leaves.

Ainsworth divided children into three categories on the basis of their reactions to the Strange Situation. The largest percentage, about two thirds, are securely attached: They cry or protest if the parent leaves the room; they welcome her back and then play happily again; they are clearly more attached to the mother than to the stranger. Other babies are insecurely attached: They may be "avoidant," not seeming to care if the mother leaves the room and making little effort to seek contact with her on her return, or "anxious and ambivalent," resisting contact with the mother at reunion but protesting loudly if she leaves. Psychologists began to worry about these children, because insecure attachment is associated with later emotional and behavioral problems, such as aggressiveness, and, in adults, with unstable, conflicted relationships.

From these beginnings, the study of attachment soon was at the center of many important social and personal questions: What does the study of baby–parent attachment teach us about adoption? Can it help resolve the Solomonic task of assigning custody in a divorce dispute? Is there a critical period in a child's early years for attachment to develop? Is there anything parents can do to assure their babies' secure attachment? If you have an insecure infant, is that your fault? If you have adopted an older child, should you try some kind of attachment therapy, and if so, what?

Jean Mercer's *Understanding Attachment* provides a secure base of historical and contemporary research on which to look for answers. Mercer, a professor of psychology and outspoken critic of unvalidated attachment therapies, shows why the notion of attachment in many popular theories of parenting is completely unrelated to the meaning of attachment in developmental psychology. She properly savages the therapy that led to the death of Candace Newmaker, although she is tolerant of "attachment parenting" and "attachment tools," methods alleged to produce happier, healthier, less crabby children—breastfeeding, "babywearing," co-sleeping, and the like. These methods have no effect on the nature of the child's attachment or later emotional development, but if parents want to practice them, Mercer says, "no harm will be done."

Mercer's summary of the policy-based implications of the empirical research on attachment is clear and useful, particularly these conclusions:

- Newborns are little affected by separation from the biological mother. The mother might be, but infants are not.

- Among children who are about 6 months of age until about age 5 years, long-term separations *are* disturbing to children and interfere with sleeping, eating, and learning. In these years, children do best in the care of consistent, responsive adults.

- By the age of five or six years, children do not suffer as much from separations and change as toddlers do. Naturally they will be sad about losses and changes in their lives, but also more resilient in coping with them. Therefore, custody decisions for children of this age or older do not need to place as much stress on the consistency of care.

Clearly a key question is: What causes insecure attachment? Ainsworth believed that the answer lay in the way mothers treat their babies during the first year. Mothers who are sensitive and responsive to their babies' needs, she said, create securely attached infants; mothers who are uncomfortable with or insensitive to their babies create insecurely attached infants. To many people, the implication was that babies needed exactly the right kind of mothering from the very first to become securely attached, a notion that caused considerable insecurity among mothers and launched an industry of advice and techniques to help reduce it.

Indeed, longitudinal studies find that if a mother is abusive, neglectful, or erratic, either because she is chronically irresponsible or clinically depressed, the child is more likely to become insecurely attached. And many babies who suffer extreme emotional

19

deprivation in their first two years later have difficulty trusting others. But nature provides infants with two compensatory factors: One is that, as far as evolution is concerned, all that matters is that babies attach to their caregivers. Evolution doesn't care if the caregiver provides lots of toys or a few, bottle-feeds or breastfeeds, leaves the baby alone for a while or wears the baby 24/7 in a sling, shares the care with other adults or older children or believes in not letting anyone else near, leaves the infant alone for hours at a stretch so that he or she will develop self-control and independence or never lets the infant alone for a nanosecond. Indeed, as evolutionary theory would predict, about two thirds of all babies become securely attached under all of these child-minding practices, all over the world.

The other compensatory factor is that most human infants are remarkably resilient. Study after study shows that the events of the first year or two do not necessarily have permanent effects. Decades ago, Emmy Werner and her associates followed more than 600 children from birth to age 32, concentrating especially on high-risk children. For some, the risks were due to biological problems such as perinatal complications or early physical difficulties; for others, the risks were due to "adverse early rearing conditions" and stressful childhood events. "As we watched these children grow from babyhood to adulthood," they reported, "we could not help but respect the self-righting tendencies within them that produced normal development under all but the most persistently adverse circumstances."

Likewise, in assessing the development of Romanian babies raised in orphanages for their first two years, Michael Rutter and his colleagues found that while these children were less likely than babies adopted earlier to become securely attached to their eventual adoptive parents, most of the children eventually adjusted perfectly well. For those who continued to have developmental problems, as Mercer observes, a lack of early attachment was not the sole reason: They were also poorly nourished, had had little or no health care, had few social contacts, and may even have had preexisting physical or mental problems that caused them to be institutionalized in the first place.

Nonetheless, in the world of attachment research, as investigators measure maternal sensitivity and environmental conditions as predictors of a child's insecure attachment, one important factor is often overlooked: the child's own genetically influenced temperament. (Mercer acknowledges this important factor only in passing but does not dwell on it or consider its implications for custody decisions or interventions.) Babies who are fearful and prone to crying from birth are more likely to show insecure behavior in the Strange Situation, regardless of how their mothers treated them. These highly reactive infants, even at four months of age, are excitable, nervous, and fearful; they overreact to any little thing. This wariness and timidity, which parents can soothe but never quite eliminate, continues throughout childhood and into adulthood; it seems to be a part of central nervous system wiring. While doing mildly stressful tasks, reactive children are more likely than nonreactive children to have increased heart rates, heightened brain activity, and high levels of stress hormones. In contrast, nonreactive infants take things easy. They lie there without fussing; they rarely cry; they babble happily. As toddlers, they are outgoing and curious about new toys and events. They continue to be easygoing and extroverted throughout childhood. They are, in a word, secure.

Thus, to understand secure attachment and resilience, researchers have found that three factors are involved: the child's own temperament, including the traits of easy-goingness and sociability; having close family ties; and, especially if those are lacking, having strong support systems outside the home. As Werner concluded, "Those who care for or work with children can help tilt the balance from vulnerability to resiliency if they accept children's temperamental idiosyncrasies" and help them develop informal but reliable attachments outside the home as well as inside it. Mercer does not talk about "children's temperamental idiosyncrasies," but they are essential in any set of guidelines for adults working with troubled children.

Secure attachments are a matter of nature and nurture, the individual and the environment. Some of the most nurturing parents in the world will have insecure children, and some secure children will survive the most erratic and troubled parents. That said, Mercer's recommendations for creating attachment-friendly daycare practices and interventions, based on the child's changing developmental needs, are smart and sensible. Attachment, like grass, will emerge through the cracks of even the hardest pavement. Whether we then water those tendrils or trample them is our choice.

21

5

■ ■ ■

Love at Goon Park
Harry Harlow and the
Science of Affection

By Deborah Blum

From the moment we are born to the end of life, we yearn for enfolding arms to comfort us. We embrace friends and loved ones in greeting and farewell, in times of joy and in times of sorrow. After any disaster, whether an earthquake or 9/11, what do strangers do? Weep and cling to one another as if to a life raft. Touch is the currency of reassurance, conversation, affection, understanding, and love.

Americans, however, have resisted acknowledging the power and importance of contact comfort. A need for touch? *Us? We* are independent, logical, rational; apart from a few loony Californians, we don't need that touchy-feely stuff. Indeed, as cross-cultural studies have shown, we are an undertouching society: The groups most in need of touch—infants, chil-dren, the aged and the sick—are often those most deprived of it.

Only in the past half century have American scientists and physicians started to understand what mothers in many cultures (such as Mayan, Italian and Japanese) have known for millen-nia: Touching is as important to health and well-being as vitamin C. As Deborah Blum shows in her superb bi-ography, *Love at Goon Park,* it was Harry Harlow who opened American eyes to the importance of human affec-tion. (The book's title refers to Harlow's laboratory at the University of Wisconsin, which was nicknamed Goon Park because the address was 600 N. Park, and a handwritten "600 N." could be misread as GOON).

I interviewed Harlow for *Psychology Today* magazine in 1972, when I was a newly minted Ph.D. and

American Scientist, March-April 2003.

he was already world-famous for research in which he raised baby monkeys with a "cloth mother" (a chicken-wire torso covered in soft terry cloth) or a food-dispensing "wire mother" (a chicken-wire frame with a milk bottle at the top). His photos of the infant monkeys, clinging for dear life to their lifeless but cuddly cloth mothers, were haunting and horrifying. Yet his work showed unequivocally that these babies—and presumably all primate babies, including human ones—needed "contact comfort" and cuddling to become attached to their mothers, thrive physically, and have normal relationships; food was not enough. In those days, that was big news.

I was pleased to reencounter Harlow, from a distance of decades, through Blum's book on the man and his work. Although he was best known for his wire-and-cloth mother studies, Harlow was a giant in twentieth-century experimental psychology, and a biography is more than warranted by his contributions to science and his place in the history of science.

Like me, Blum was fascinated by his lively but troubled personality and his important but often cruel research. In my conversation with Harlow, we wrangled about the ethics of his research—the brutality, in one project, of separating infant monkeys from their mothers and keeping them in terrified isolation—and about his provocatively sexist remarks. "If you don't believe that God created women to be mothers and essentially nothing else," he said to me, "let me prove it to you." The proof consisted of a description of sex differences in monkey behavior, and then he finished triumphantly with the one sex difference he was sure of: "Man is the only animal capable of speaking, and woman is the only animal incapable of not speaking."

This was vintage Harry Harlow, unapologetically inflammatory before the term *political correctness* had been coined. He delighted in baiting me, a young woman coming of professional age during a rebirth of feminism; yet it seemed to me, even then, that he did so in a spirit of intellectual playfulness and provocation rather than meanness. Indeed, Blum shows that Harlow's sexist remarks and jokes seemed to be intended to rile people up and tease them rather than to be a reflection of some truly felt misogyny. In practice, where it counted, his male and female students received equal treatment—that is, he was equally demanding of everyone. He liked strong, independent female students and supported their careers.

Blum feels the same ambivalence about her subject that I did. Was he someone one could like? "Easy question, tricky answer," she says in her preface:

> He makes me laugh, even second-hand. He makes me think about friendship and parenthood and partnership in ways that I never had before. He still seems to me an edgy companion. And he seems wholly real. So, like Harry, the answer is complicated. Sometimes I do like him, sometimes not at all. In the end—it's the both that makes him such a terrific subject for a biography— exasperating, sometimes, enchant-

23

ing other times, never boring. And his weaknesses give a curious strength to his work—he was bitterly honest, sometimes to his own detriment. He was willing to take his personal problems—loneliness and isolation and depression, even—and use them in his research.

This paragraph illustrates why this book is so good both as a contribution to the history of science and as a biography. Blum avoids the twin temptations of hero worship and character assassination. She gives us the strengths and weaknesses of Harlow's character and work, placing both in the context of what was happening in psychology and in the larger culture. Harlow made many discoveries that were pioneering, indeed heretical, at the time: that monkeys use tools, solve problems, and learn and explore because they are curious or interested in something, not just to get food or other rewards. But his greatest contribution was his demonstration of the power of "mother love" and contact comfort, and the devastation that ensues when an infant is untouched, unloved, neglected.

Was Harlow the first to demonstrate this need? No, both René Spitz and John Bowlby had, much earlier, shown how infants raised in orphanages, where they were fed but never cuddled, sickened and failed to thrive. Was experimenting with monkeys, by raising them in isolation with only wire or cloth "mothers" and causing them anguish that no observer could fail to see, essential to make the same point? Probably not. I feel about

Harlow's studies as I did about Stanley Milgram's famous studies of obedience to authority, in which large numbers of people inflicted what they believed to be serious pain on another person because the experimenter told them to. Did we not have enough examples from history to confirm that, as C. P. Snow observed, "more hideous crimes have been committed in the name of obedience ... than in the name of rebellion"? What Harlow and Milgram were able to do, however, was to make the case for their findings dramatic, compelling and *scientifically incontrovertible.* Their evidence was based not on anecdote, however persuasive the story, but on solid, empirical, replicated data. As Blum shows, that's what it took to begin to undermine a scientific worldview in which the need for touch and cuddling—physical expressions of mother love—was ignored.

Love at Goon Park is utterly devoid of the post-hoc psychodynamic reasoning that is the hallmark of most journalists and many historians who attempt psychological biographies. Blum has written an invaluable story for all students of psychological science, for she shows how science is *really* done and how its findings are used and often misused. Scientific discoveries are a result not only of a bloodless progression from hypothesis to experiment to refinements, but also of the investigator's personality and passions, and of lucky accidents—who happened to be where, who was lucky enough to work with whom. Science also depends on knowing when to follow your hunches and when to change direction, and on knowing the difference between an obstacle in your path and a dead end. Blum brings all of these elements of scientific discovery to life in Harlow's story.

Blum shows that in spite of Harlow's difficult personality, his drinking problems and his bouts of severe depression, he was the consummate scientist and mentor, supporting his students through good ideas and failures. His graduate student Leonard Rosenblum had been working on an experiment that involved building a large, complicated maze that would allow him to measure the social and intellectual behavior of monkeys. Rosenblum worked for months with no results, and one day Harlow came by and said, "Rosenblum, take a sledgehammer to that thing and get rid of it.... You've got to know when to quit." Rosenblum was shocked but realized Harlow was right. "If you cling to errors, you never learn the right way. It was a very difficult lesson," Rosenblum told Blum. "I was embarrassed and ashamed. But he didn't see it that way." Rosenblum went on to devise a crucial variation of Harlow's paradigm, raising infant monkeys with the chance to play regularly with their age mates. These babies grew up to be as socially healthy as those raised with real mothers.

A general problem in the text is Blum's tendency to imply that the bad old days of narrow-minded, misguided psychological advice are past. We understand, we say, so much more about the importance of bonding, contact, and attachment! Yes, we do, but we are no less vulnerable to today's social pressures and cultural values, or to the misuse of science on behalf of vested interests—especially the many vested emotional, political, and economic interests involved in contemporary child-rearing practices and notions of correct mothering.

In Blum's hands, Harry Harlow emerges, for all his flaws, as the kind of scientist who is an endangered species: willing to speak his mind and speak it clearly, free of cant or jargon, no matter whom his remarks offended; willing to follow his data where it took him, even against the tides of popular opinion. He would never get tenure today.

6

■■■

Happiness
Lessons from a New Science

By Richard Layard

Making Happy People
The Nature of Happiness and Its Origins in Childhood

By Paul Martin

Going Sane

By Adam Phillips

I n the early 1970s, when a friend and I were newly hatched social psychologists, we decided to write a book on happiness. The head of an eminent Boston publishing house took pity on us and, over lunch, explained the facts of life. "No one wants to read a book on happiness," he said kindly. "Happy people don't; why in the world would they want to? They are

Times Literary Supplement, June 17, 2005.

already happy. Unhappy people don't want to, either. Why in the world would they want to read about happy people when they are feeling sullen and miserable? Moreover, it's faintly embarrassing to be seen on a bus or park bench reading a book on happiness. It's like being caught reading a book on pedophilia. A passerby will question your motives." And so my friend and I went our separate ways; he to write a book on loneliness, and I, a book on anger.

But time and psychology have marched on, and now we are in the midst of, if not of a happiness epidemic, a happiness-book epidemic. The positive psychology movement, a contemporary incarnation of its humanist predecessors (though its proponents will wrestle you to the ground denying their heritage, as children will do), is again eager to help people reach their "fullest potential," as Abraham Maslow advocated in the 1960s. This time around, however, the movement has produced a wave of research on who is happy, who isn't, and why. These researchers often manage to hold their professional meetings in places like Bermuda in the winter, which suggests that positive psychologists know how to practice what they preach. Warmth in winter is a fine contribution to contentment.

An inherent but debatable assumption in positive psychology is that happiness is a quality that can be fostered or suppressed, raised or lowered, by the conditions of our lives, our choices, and our mental habits. There is considerable evidence, however, that each of us has something like a happiness thermostat that keeps us bubbling along at the level we were set to be. It drops during extreme conditions (war, violence, bereavement, poverty) and rises during times of celebration, but otherwise remains steady in a middle range.

Daniel Gilbert, a professor of psychology at Harvard and author of *Stumbling on Happiness*, has found that most people assume that they will be emotionally devastated by misfortune, and so they overestimate the intensity and duration of breakups, divorces, financial losses, insults, injuries, and trauma. People do suffer from these experiences, but eventually most return to normal, and sooner than they would have believed. "Our ability to spin gold from the dross of our experience means that we often find ourselves flourishing in circumstances we once dreaded," Gilbert says. "We fear divorces, natural disasters and financial hardships until they happen, at which point we recognize them as opportunities to reinvent ourselves, to bond with our neighbors and to transcend the spiritual poverty of material excess." Most of us are basically happy, in other words, unless we suffer from chronic depression or are afflicted with the personality disposition that behavioral geneticists call "negative affectivity," a tendency to be crabby, complaining, bitter, and irritable no matter what happens.

Richard Layard, an economist and member of the House of Lords, and Paul Martin, a behavioral biologist, have both produced cheerful, optimistic books that dispute this view of happiness. Marshalling studies of the social, psychological, economic, cognitive, and neurological contributions to happiness, they make a case for building a society that can improve the happiness and well-being of its citizens as well as their material security. Layard dispenses with definitions. By happiness, he means "feeling good—enjoying life and wanting the feeling to be maintained. By unhappiness I mean feeling bad and wishing things were different." (He does not consider those of us who feel good *and* wish things were different.) Paul Martin gets closer by defining happiness as a combination of pleasure, the absence of unpleasant emotions and pain, and the judgment that one's life is good. In his view, happiness consists of neither the mindless pursuit of pleasure nor of Spinoza's insensate "rational understanding of life and the world," but a blend of good feeling and smart thinking. It is more than the absence of unhappiness just as health is more than the absence of disease—or, as Adam Phillips would add, just as sanity is more than the absence of insanity.

Both books make the case that happy people feel better, achieve more, create more, enjoy better health, live longer, and make better friends and partners than the gloomy misanthropes among us. (Societies also need people who are depressed, anxious, angry, and rebellious, however, as they are often the source of creativity, art, and social change.) Martin lists the factors that contribute to happiness, but because the positive psychology people tend to study attributes rather than individuals ("do happy people feel more in control of their lives than unhappy people?"), it's a long and overlapping list:

Connectedness, social and emotional competence, freedom from anxiety, communication skills, meaningful activity, a sense of control, a sense of purpose and meaning, resilience, self-esteem, optimism, having an outward focus, humor, playfulness, wisdom, and "flow," engagement in an activity for its own sake. Also, it helps to get a good night's sleep and exercise regularly. Oh, and also it's good if you can avoid spending too many hours commuting to work. And wait, education is critically important, too. After reading all of these ingredients of happiness, the reader may feel a need to simplify—say, by taking a nap or having a nice cup of tea and a scone, my own brief afternoon bliss.

It's tempting to make fun of happiness books; they are such an easy target, soft and plump, just asking to be pinched. The new ones have the imprimatur of science on observations that have been made for centuries: Money can't buy happiness; human beings need social bonds, satisfying work, and strong communities; there is nothing good or bad but thinking makes it so; a life based entirely on the pursuit of money and pleasure ultimately becomes pleasureless. Layard and Martin's work, however, has the virtue of asking readers to think about why it is that, given what we know makes us happy, we consistently organize our lives and make choices that make us unhappy.

The problem is comparable to the worldwide epidemic of obesity. Evolution has seen to it that most human beings gain weight when food is easily available, tasty, rich, varied, and cheap, as it is in all developed

28

nations today. When diets consist of the same food day after day, people habituate to what they are eating and eat less of it. As soon as food becomes more varied, people eat more and gain more weight. What then should be done, if anything, about obesity as a public health problem? Some individuals are able to summon the will power to change their eating habits, but will power won't go far on a global scale, not with the proliferation of the high-calorie, cheap fast food that humans love to eat, that the poor can afford, that many cultures equate with nurturance, and that makes billions for its marketers.

With happiness as with food, what is good for human beings right this minute, what feels good in the short run, is not always what is good over time. Consider television, which is to happiness what McDonald's is to slenderness. People enjoy television for many reasons, and even infants will turn to its rapidly changing colorful images like a plant to sun. In excess, television promotes passivity and anxiety, filling time that people might otherwise spend on activities that are intrinsically satisfying and create a sense of competence. Yet, given a choice, many people choose television and other narcotic pleasures that dull the mind and quell its restless search for meaning over activities that, in their complexity and challenge, offer the real promise of satisfaction. Likewise, the ubiquity of advertising, the engine that drives the marketplace, creates a craving for material things that promise happiness. The new thing does so, for a while; then the purchaser habituates to the

thing, and soon needs another thing to boost happiness. The resulting "hedonic treadmill" keeps people reaching for a state of happiness that will never arrive.

Is this dilemma best left to each individual to handle or is it one that governments should tackle? Both Martin and Layard believe that governments can and should do more. "A radical pro-happiness government would acknowledge that rampant consumerism and advertising undermine unhappiness," Martin argues, "and it might even consider using taxation or regulation to discourage them." There's a radical concept! Layard takes it further, proposing that government should make the happiness of its citizens a primary goal, the heart of its public and economic policy, using laws and taxes to reward cooperation in pursuit of a common good, make work life more compatible with family life, help the poor, reduce rates of mental illness, subsidize activities that promote "community life," reduce commuting time, eliminate high unemployment, prohibit commercial advertising to children (as Sweden does).... If the thermostat theory is right, none of this will raise the overall happiness level of the population, and some temperamentally grouchy people will complain that they miss the traffic, but who cares? Sign me up.

The reason that social scientists have studied the negative side of human behavior far more often than the positive side is apparent in Adam Phillips's *Going Sane*. If happiness is elusive, sanity is evanescent. "There is something about the whole notion of sanity that seems to make us averse to defining it," writes Phillips. Could it be because sanity isn't an "it"? Social scientists and psychiatrists can define and measure the many emotions that are incompatible with happiness (grief, bitterness, melancholy, worry, and their kin) and the mental disorders they might agree are incompatible with sanity (schizophrenia and other psychoses). But the reason they have shied away from defining and measuring "normal" happiness and sanity is that these are moral and philosophic concepts, not psychological or medical ones.

"Sanities should be elaborated in the way that diagnoses of pathology are," Phillips suggests; "they should be contested like syndromes, debated as to their causes and contributions and outcomes, exactly as illnesses are." Having left this daunting task to others, he ends up speaking of "the superficially sane" and the "deeply sane," whatever that distinction means. The book is full of the kind of psychoanalytic generalizations that may cause the reader temporary insanity: "So the sane have a sense that anything they want is either going to frustrate them because it isn't quite what they really want; or it is going to horrify them because it is more nearly what they want, and so they will be unable to enjoy it."

Happiness and sanity? Let's be glad we know them when we feel them, and concentrate instead on ways of reducing pain, anguish, and rage. Succeeding in that effort will do as much for human happiness as penicillin did for human health.

7

■ ■ ■

Bright-Sided

How the Relentless Promotion of Positive Thinking has Undermined America

(published in Great Britain as Smile or Die:
How positive thinking fooled America and the world*)*
by Barbara Ehrenreich

In 2007 I read Barbara Ehrenreich's essay in *Harper's* about her experience being treated for breast cancer. It felt like a bracing blast of clean, cool air in a musty room. It was not about her medical treatment but about the infantilizing breast-cancer-survivor industry, with its pink ribbons, teddy bears, and relentless cheerfulness. You may not call yourself a victim or a patient; you must see yourself as a "survivor." You must not be angry or raise any pesky political questions about the dismal state of health care in America or possible environmental causes of cancer. You must not whine or cry, because negative emotions and attitudes are not only a sign of psychological defeat, but also a sure way to make the cancer return or grow faster. If it does return, it's your fault for not being positive enough and thinking the right thoughts. Ehrenreich is furious at the burden that this erroneous belief places on patients, as revealed in one woman's statement, "I know that if I get sad, scared or upset, I am making my tumor grow faster and I will have shortened my life." Smile or die, indeed.

Barbara Ehrenreich has long been a tireless fighter against the purveyors

Times Literary Supplement, May 14, 2010.

of silliness and self-deception who clog America's airwaves and best-seller lists, reserving special venom for those who profit by taking advantage of the poor, the unemployed, the uninsured. In books such as *Nickel and Dimed: On (not) getting by in America* and *Bait and Switch: On the (futile) pursuit of the American dream*, she reminded readers to ask who benefits when Americans who are struggling financially are advised to solve their problems by wishing harder and praying more—and that if they do, they will become rich too. In *Smile or Die*, she takes on the excesses, delusions, and unsupported promises of the positive-thinking movement, tracking both its naïve and its corrupt incarnations in the worlds of health, business, religion, and psychology.

"Positive thinking" is the shmoo of American culture: an irresistible target that invites mockery but is impossible to eradicate. (The shmoo, a cartoon character invented by Al Capp in 1948, would do anything to make you happy, absorb any abuse you cared to hurl at it, and then, if you were hungry, turn itself into a nice steak dinner for you.) Ehrenreich examines the rise of positive thinking from its inception in the nineteenth century, where it began as a revolt against dour Calvinism's fulminations about hard work and eternal damnation. Mary Baker Eddy's invention of Christian Science, allied with Phineas Quimby's New Thought movement, held that illness was all in the mind, and therefore, a Mind Cure was better than a medical one. (In many cases, given the state of medicine at the time, it was.) What Mary Baker Eddy was

to the nineteenth century, Norman Vincent Peale was to the twentieth; his *The Power of Positive Thinking* in turn spawned legions of best sellers, such as Rhonda Byrne's *The Secret*, whose secret is that if you are poor, unhappy, or jobless, the fault lies not in your stars or your circumstances but in your thoughts.

What a welcome message for companies busily laying off employees! Between 1981 and 2003, some thirty million full-time American workers lost their jobs as corporations downsized. As that happened, Ehrenreich argues, positive thinking became a big business, and big business was its principal client. Corporations, having no safety nets to offer their laid-off workers, offered psychological cheerleading instead: How better to manage workers' despair and head off anger than by hiring motivational speakers to give them pep talks about all the new opportunities they now had? Don't be angry at your boss or blame the system, advises Zig Ziglar, a Christian motivational speaker, "work harder and pray more."

Unfortunately, corporations bought the message of positive thinking themselves: "Why bother worrying about dizzying levels of debt and exposure to potential defaults," Ehrenreich writes, "when all good things come to those who are optimistic enough to expect them?" Ehrenreich knows that the economic collapse that struck America has many complex causes, but she argues that positive thinking paved the road to disaster as American corporate culture replaced "the dreary rationality of professional management" with cheery expectations of ever-greater success. They were victims of the same delusional thinking they sold to their workers: wishing will make it so. Don't bother me with your grumpy, pessimistic reminders that bubbles always burst. There's money to be made right now.

Ehrenreich is at full speed by the time she takes on positive psychology, a movement within academic psychology that investigates "the science of happiness" (see Essay 6). She interviews one of the founders of the movement, Martin Seligman, who, perhaps aware of her skepticism, does his best to elude her probing questions. Ehrenreich gives him a hard time about his Authentic Happiness questionnaire, on which she scored a "less-than-jubilant 3.67 out of 5," mostly because she didn't feel "extraordinarily proud" of herself and confessed to being pessimistic about the future—"assuming that it was the future of our species at issue, not just my own."

Unlike many of the unskeptical reporters who have interviewed researchers in the positive-psychology field, Ehrenreich has done her homework, examining the data beneath the claims and learning that many of those claims are tenuous or wrong:

- Optimism does not prolong life.
- Support groups do not affect the course of cancer.
- Among older people who lose a loved one, pessimists are less likely to become depressed than optimists.
- People who are grumpy and neurotic "do more complaining about

angina but are at no greater risk of pathology than cheerful people."
- Happy people do not have "feistier immune systems than less happy people," as Seligman once said.

Many of the researchers in this field are scrupulously careful in their professional writings, by noting, as one team did, "serious conceptual and methodological reservations" about the literature on positive emotions and health, the inconsistent findings, and even the "potentially harmful" effects of some of the research. Yet when most of them speak to reporters or general audiences, or write popular books, they admit that they often get "ahead of the science." They oversimplify, smoothing away those pesky inconsistencies and negative findings. (The media and the major funder of research in positive psychology, the conservative Templeton Foundation, want positive results about positive thinking.) Seligman says that within a decade "we'll have self-help books that actually work." Given that he has already written one, this curious remark suggests he is practicing some positive thinking himself.

Ehrenreich may be forgiven for not knowing the origins of positive psychology within the field, but Seligman and his colleagues should know better. They almost never acknowledge their debt to Abraham Maslow and Carl Rogers, who, in the 1960s, argued that it was time for a "third force" in American psychology— humanism, an alternative to then-dominant world views of psychoanalysis and behaviorism. Humanists wanted psychologists to pay more attention to the positive aspects of life, including joy, humor, love, and the rare moments of rapture caused by the attainment of excellence or the experience of beauty. Most of the humanists were not scientists themselves, but they spurred research on such admirable attributes as empathy, courage, resilience, altruism, the motivation to excel, and self-confidence. This was the kind of positive psychology Ehrenreich would welcome, as her own book *Dancing in the Streets: A history of collective joy* suggests. Ehrenreich is in favor of joy.

Like all warriors with a take-no-prisoners approach to a problem, however, she occasionally sweeps some innocent civilians into her net. Because Ehrenreich's goal is to lay waste to all aspects of reality-denying, self-defeating, and otherwise goofy forms of positive thinking across society, she does not separate the wheat from the chaff, and thereby loses some wheat. For one thing, the basic premise of positive thinking is neither new nor American: The Stoic philosophy that negative, destructive emotions are created by our thoughts and errors of judgment flourished three hundred years B.C. The contemporary practice of cognitive behavioral therapy is based on this notion, and it has been supported by hundreds of empirical studies.

Further, decades of research in social psychology have shown that the attitude Ehrenreich finds so saccharine and typically American—the remarks that many cancer patients make to the effect that "I'm a different and better person now"—reflects the universal human need to reduce the dissonance between "something horrible has happened to me" and "how do I make sense of this?" Worldwide, most people answer that question by saying "I'm stronger for it"; "God willed this"; "God is testing me"; "This brush with death caused me to change my values and become a better person." Likewise, health psychologists have shown the emotional benefits of what they call downward social comparisons: "I have cancer, but thank God it's not Lou Gehrig's disease, which is far worse." These forms of positive thinking do not make people healthier, but they do relieve anxiety and despair. And there is nothing uniquely American about them; they reflect a touching facet of human resilience.

But what is uniquely American is the way that motivational entrepreneurs, religious hucksters, and psychologists willing to jump "ahead of the science" have packaged and sold positive thinking as a commodity, as if it were a tonic that can bring us safety, security, and health all on its own. "The threats we face are real and can be vanquished only by shaking off self-absorption and taking action in the world," Ehrenreich writes. And that requires thinking critically as well as positively.

8

■ ■ ■

The Nurture Assumption

Why Children Turn Out the Way They Do

By Judith Rich Harris

As I was writing this review, two friends called to ask me about "that book that says parents don't matter." Well, that's not what it says. What *The Nurture Assumption* does say about parents and children, however, warrants the lively controversy it began generating even before publication.

Judith Rich Harris was chucked out of graduate school at Harvard on the grounds that she was unlikely to become a proper experimental psychologist. She never became an academic and instead turned her hand to writing textbooks in developmental psychology. From this bird's-eye vantage point, she began to question widespread belief in the "nurture as-sumption—the notion that parents are the most important part of a child's environment and can determine, to a large extent, how the child turns out." She believes that parents must share credit (or blame) with the child's own temperament, and, most of all with the child's peers. "The world that children share with their peers is what shapes their behavior and modifies the characteristics they were born with," Harris writes, "and hence determines the sort of people they will be when they grow up."

The public may be forgiven for saying, "Here we go again." One year we're told bonding is the key, the next that it's birth order. Wait, what really matters is stimulation. The first five years of life are the most important; no, the first three years; no, it's all over by the first year. Forget that: It's all genetics! Cancel those baby massage sessions!

What makes Harris's book important is that it puts all these theories into larger perspective, showing what each contributes and where it is flawed. Some critics may pounce on her for not having a Ph.D. or an academic position, and others will quarrel with the importance she places on peers and genes, but they cannot fault her scholarship. Harris is not generalizing from a single study that can be attacked on statistical grounds, or even from a single field; she draws on research from behavior genetics (the study of genetic contributions to personality), social psychology, child development, ethology, evolution and culture. Lively anecdotes about real children suffuse this book, but Harris never confuses anecdotes with data. The originality of *The Nurture Assumption* lies not in the studies she cites, but in the way she has reconfigured them to explain findings that have puzzled psychologists for years.

First, researchers have been unable to find any child-rearing practice that predicts children's personalities, achievements, or problems outside the home. Parents don't have a single child-rearing style anyway, because how they treat their children depends largely on what the children are like. They are more permissive with easy children and more punitive with defiant ones.

Second, even when parents do treat their children the same way, the children turn out differently. The majority of children of troubled and even abusive parents are resilient and do not suffer lasting psychological damage. Conversely, many children of the kindest and most nurturing parents succumb to drugs, mental illness, or gangs.

Third, there is no correlation—zero—between the personality traits of adopted children and their adoptive parents or other children in the home, as there should be if home environment had a strong influence.

Fourth, how children are raised—in day care or at home, with one parent or two, with gay parents or straight ones, with an employed mom or one who stays home—has little or no influence on children's personalities.

Finally, what parents do with and for their children affects children mainly when they are with their parents. For instance, mothers influence their children's play only while the children are playing with them; when the child is playing alone or with a playmate, it makes no difference what games mom played with them.

Most psychologists have done what anyone would do when faced with this astonishing, counterintuitive evidence: They have tried to dismiss it. Yet eventually the most unlikely idea wins if it has the evidence to back it up. As psychologist Carole Wade puts it, trying to squeeze existing facts into an outdated theory is like trying to fit a double-sized sheet onto a queen-sized bed. One corner fits, but another pops out. You need a new sheet or a new bed.

The Nurture Assumption is a new sheet, one that covers the discrepant facts. I don't agree with all the author's claims and interpretations;

often she reaches too far to make her case, throwing the parent out with the bath water, as it were. But such criticisms should not detract from her accomplishment, which is to give us a richer, more accurate portrait of how children develop than we have had from outdated Freudianism or piecemeal research.

The first problem with the nurture assumption is nature. The findings of behavior genetics show, incontrovertibly, that many personality traits and abilities have a genetic component. No news here; many others have reported this research, notably the psychologist Jerome Kagan in *The Nature of the Child*. But genes explain only about half of the variation in people's personalities and abilities. What's the other half?

Harris's brilliant stroke was to change the discussion from nature (genes) and nurture (parents) to its older version: heredity and environment. "Environment" is broader than nurture. Children, like adults, have two environments: their homes and their world outside the home; their behavior, like ours, changes depending on the situation they are in. Many parents know the eerie experience of having their child's teacher describe their child in terms they barely recognize (*"my* kid did *what?"*). Children who fight with their siblings may be placid with friends. They can be honest at home and deceitful at school, or vice versa. At home children learn how their parents want them to behave and what they can get away with; but, Harris shows, "These patterns of behavior are not like albatrosses that we have to drag along with us wherever we go, all through our lives. We don't even drag them to nursery school."

Harris has taken a factor, peers, that everyone acknowledges is important, but instead of treating it as a nuisance in children's socialization, she makes it a major player. Children are merciless in persecuting a kid who is different—one who says "Warshington" instead of "Washington," one who has a foreign accent or wears the wrong clothes. Parents have long lamented the apparent cruelty of children and the obsessive conformity of teenagers, but, Harris argues, they have missed the point: Children's attachment to their peer groups is not irrational, it's essential. It is evolution's way of seeing to it that kids bond with each other, fit in and survive. Identification with the peer group, not identification with the parent, is the key to human survival. That is why children have their own traditions, words, rules, games; their culture operates in opposition to adult rules. Their goal is not to become successful adults but successful children. Teenagers want to excel as teen-agers, which means being unlike adults.

It has been difficult to tease apart the effects of parents and peers, Harris observes, because children's environments often duplicate parental values, language and customs. (Indeed, many parents see to it that they do.) To see what factors are strongest, therefore, we must look at situations in which these environments clash. For example, when parents value academic achievement and a student's peers do not, who wins? Typically, peers. Differences between black and white teenagers in achievement have

37

variously been attributed to genes, social class, or single mothers, but differences vanish when researchers control for the peer group: whether its members value achievement and expect to go to college, or regard academic success as a hopeless dream or sellout to "white" values.

Are there exceptions? Of course, and Harris anticipates them. Some children in anti-intellectual peer groups choose the lonely path of nerdy devotion to schoolwork. And some have the resources, from genes or parents, to resist peer pressure. But exceptions should not detract from the rule: that children, like adults, are oriented to their peers. Do you dress, think, and behave more like others of your generation, your parents, or the current crop of young teenagers?

Harris writes beautifully, in a tone both persuasive and conversational. But many people are deeply invested, financially and emotionally, in the "nurture assumption" and won't give it up without a fight: the vast advice-to-parents industry and the "guilty mother" brigade, whose work fills our airwaves, books, magazines, and newspapers; therapists who believe that our personalities and problems are created by unconscious dynamics, neurotic parents, or childhood experiences; politicians elected on the claims that day care, divorce, and working mothers are bad for children; and people who want to blame their parents for everything that's wrong in their lives.

Others, however, may reject this book because of concerns about its potential misuses. If it is natural for children to exclude outsiders, why should schools make any effort to integrate children of different ethnicities, sexes, or abilities? Why should we pay for prenatal care or better schools if smart, resilient kids will turn out all right whatever we do, and troubled ones will be lost to deviant peer groups?

These concerns are especially important in the United States, which lags behind European nations in measures supporting children's health, education, and universal day care. Some people may indeed try to use Harris's evidence to legitimize our national neglect of children. For those committed to the well-being of all children, however, here is information that can lead to better programs, ones that might actually work.

For example, Harris makes it clear why most bilingual education programs have failed: Children will speak the way their friends do. If other kids are speaking the language they hear at home, that's what they'll speak. If other kids speak English with a Spanish or Bostonian accent, they will acquire an accent too. If other kids are speaking a language they don't know, they'll learn it fast. Any program, bilingual or monolingual, that doesn't take into account the power of peers is doomed. Likewise, Harris shows why the costly programs designed to get teen-agers to avoid drugs, stay in school, or abstain from sex have been such duds; they have been targeted to individual teenagers or their parents.

The greatest fear surrounding Harris's book is that her message will somehow encourage the neglect or outright abuse of children. This concern reveals, perhaps, what a deeply antichild culture we are, for it assumes that we are nice to children only out of a desire to make them perfect replicas of ourselves, and if we can't do that, we might as well abandon them. But if you realize that you can't turn your shy child into an extrovert, does that mean you won't help her cope in scary new situations? Why should the good news that most children are resilient be construed in any way as an endorsement of neglecting their health or permitting adults to abuse them?

Harris believes that parents should treat children well for the reason they should be kind to their partners, not in hopes of transforming their personalities or controlling their futures but in hopes of remaining good friends for a lifetime. Parents matter, she says, primarily in determining the kind of relationship they will have with their children—friendly or bitter, accepting or adversarial—and how their children feel about them.

Many readers will disagree with Harris's conclusions about the limited influence of parents. Everyone knows people who have spent untold hours with their shy, difficult, or learning-disabled children (genetic predispositions all) and thereby helped their children succeed in their peer groups, school, and life. And everyone has friends whose harsh, unforgiving, or neglectful parents left wounds that still hurt, though these wounds might never be apparent on a personality test.

Yet it would be a shame if readers get so focused on the degree to which parents matter that they overlook Harris's most important message, which is that parents aren't *all* that matter. This news should reassure people who blame themselves, as society blames them, for their children's problems with drugs, mental illness, or violence. But it may panic parents who are consumed by a near-hysterical passion to control their children's personalities, abilities, careers, safety, and eating habits, and inspire them to start feverishly trying to micromanage their children's peer groups as well. Forget it. "The idea that we can make our children turn out any way we want is an illusion," Harris writes. "You can neither perfect them nor ruin them. They are not yours to perfect or ruin: they belong to tomorrow." In current cacophony of advice to parents, could any words be wiser?

9

■ ■ ■

Personality
What Makes You the Way You Are

By Daniel Nettle

What a difference a century makes. One hundred years ago, Sigmund Freud's answer to Daniel Nettle's question in his subtitle, "What makes you the way you are?", would have begun with your unconscious mind: the unique pattern of fantasies, defenses, and instinctual conflicts that create your neurotic insecurities and self-defeating habits. These unconscious mechanisms would, in turn, have been profoundly influenced by your parents, who overpunished you or underappreciated you, who told you too much about sex or not enough. You can't do much about your personality, though you can tweak it a bit with years of psychoanalysis.

Today, personality researchers almost uniformly agree that the answer to "what makes you the way you are?" is a combination of your genes, your peers, and the idiosyncratic, chance experiences that befall you in childhood and adulthood. Your parents influence your relationship with them—loving or contentious, conflicted or close—but not your "personality," that package of traits we label extroverted or shy, bitter or friendly, hostile or warm, gloomy or optimistic. Your genes, not your parents, are the reason you think that parachuting yourself out of airplanes is fun, or, conversely, that you feel sick to the stomach at the mere idea of doing such a crazy thing voluntarily. You can't do much about your personality, though you can tweak it a bit with cognitive therapy.

Freud's view of personality was passionate, controversial, sexy, unfalsifiable, and wrong. But it was a *personal* theory of personality. Anyone could immediately apply it, party-game style, to his or her own

Times Literary Supplement, April 18, 2008.

unconscious motivations, hidden fantasies, and terrible parents. The behavioral-genetics view of personality is calm, uncontroversial (except to a few diehard Freudians), empirically testable, and correct. But it is an *impersonal* theory of personality. Oh, shoot, genes? How sexy is that? Everyone has genes. Let me tell you about my mother...

Daniel Nettle takes on the task of showing how evolution and genetics have conspired to create "wanderers, worriers, controllers, empathizers, and poets," along with daredevils and wallflowers. Gone are the old type theories (are you a Thinking or Feeling type?) and single-trait descriptors (do you have a Machiavellian personality? Are you an erotophobe or an erotophile?). Evolutionary theory, the genome project, studies of identical twins reared together and apart, and brain-imaging techniques such as PET scans and fMRIs have given scientists the theory and methods of identifying the differences in how people's nervous systems are wired up and how those differences express themselves in characteristic responses to other people and to events.

These characteristic responses statistically cluster into into five basic factors, which are pretty much the same in every culture that has been studied, from Britain to Korea, Ethiopia to Japan, China to the Czech Republic. Nettle spends a chapter apiece on each of the five: *extraversion*, the extent to which a person is outgoing, talkative, adventurous, and sociable or shy, silent, reclusive, and cautious; *neuroticism*, the extent to which a person suffers from anxiety and other negative emotions such as anger, guilt, worry, and resentment; *agreeableness*, the extent to which a person is good-natured, cooperative, and nonjudgmental, or irritable, abrasive, and suspicious; *conscientiousness*, the extent to which a person is responsible, persevering, self-disciplined, and tidy, or undependable, quick to give up, fickle, sloppy, and careless; and *openness to experience*, the extent to which a person is curious, imaginative, questioning, and creative, or conforming, unimaginative, predictable, and uncomfortable with novelty.

You know these people, don't you? You can see yourself in this list, can't you? But if you are worrying that you are genetically disposed to worrying, don't worry about it. Each of these dimensions, Nettle shows, has, in evolutionary terms, benefits and costs. Extroverts may risk their necks to forage for food in strange places, but they are also more likely than their cautious peers to be eaten by strange creatures. Agreeable people may have harmonious relationships, but by putting others first, they may lose status and opportunities to advance. Neurotics are more vulnerable to anxiety and depression and they see clouds in every silver lining; but they are also hypervigilant to dangers in the environment, some of which, after all, are realistic.

As evolutionary theory would predict, you don't have to be a person to have a personality. Four of the five factors (apart from conscientiousness, a cognitively complex trait) have been identified in more than 60 species, not only in our fellow primates but also in bears, dogs, pigs, hyenas, goats, cats, and even the octopus. For anyone wondering how researchers study octopus personality, the answer is simple. They drop dinner (a crab) into a tank of octopuses and watch what they do. Some octopuses will aggressively grab their dinner at once. Some are more passive and wait for the crab to swim near them. And some are devious; they wait and attack the crab when no one is watching. These personality dispositions among octopuses can be reliably identified by independent observers.

Nettle also explains why evolution hasn't made life easy for itself by simply selecting for one kind of trait among members of a species. Some guppies, for example, are more wary than others. Put them in a tank with one of their natural predators, such as "the splendidly named pumpkinseed," and in only 24 hours, 14 of 20 highly wary guppies will still be alive, compared to only 5 of the 20 unwary, extroverted guppies. Shouldn't evolution have seen to it, then, that wariness would become a universal guppy trait, akin to the long neck of the giraffe? No, because guppies live in different environments. If you are a guppy in a pumpkinseed-free environment, you don't want to be wasting your time searching for predators when you could be dating and mating (an activity that in humans, if not guppies, requires its own degree of wariness). Most environments provide a constantly changing level of danger from predators, making it maximally beneficial for any group of guppies to be grateful to have both cautious members and bold ones.

Behavioral-genetic studies have consistently found that the heritability of personality traits, whether the Big Five or one of many others from aggressiveness to happiness, is around 50. This means that within a group of people, about 50 percent of the variation in such traits is attributable to genetic differences among the individuals in the group. Most people have assumed that the other 50 percent comes from the shared environment of the home: parental child-rearing methods and the experiences the child shares with siblings and parents. If it did, studies should find a strong correlation between the personality traits of adopted children and those of their adoptive parents. In fact, the correlation is weak to nonexistent. This means that when children resemble their parents and grandparents temperamentally, it is because they share genes with these relatives, not experiences. What, then, is going on in the unshared environment, the other half of the influences that make us the way we are?

Basically, Nettles argues, we don't know. "The area of environmental influences on personality is a morass of unsupported or poorly tested ideas," Nettle observes. He suggests that the reason there is only one Daniel Nettle, not 200 Daniel Nettles who are "also working on books about the five-factor model of personality," is that the five factors can be channeled in countless ways, encouraged or impeded given a person's chance experiences, opportunities, health, peers, and immediate circumstances. Moreover, because human beings, unlike the guppy and the octopus, have complex, sense-making minds, they are forever telling stories about themselves to explain why they are the way they are. No one else will experience Nettle's life as he does or interpret it as he does. Our story-telling brains make each of us unique.

When Judith Rich Harris reported the same information about the genetic origins of personality in her pioneering book *The Nurture Assumption* (see Essay 8) and then developed a richly complex theory about the origins of individual differences in *No Two Alike* (2007), readers understood that we are in the midst of an intellectual revolution about what makes us the way we are. Nettle, in contrast, has written an engaging primer on the genetics of personality, but he does not fully examine the implications of this work for child rearing, parent-blaming, literary analysis, memoir, psychotherapy and human hubris. Were he to have done so, readers would have more deeply felt the impact and consequences of coming to the end of the Freudian story, and of being at the exhilarating start of a new one.

10

■■■

"Are Girls As Mean As Books Say They Are?"

Works Cited in This Essay:

Rachel Simmons, *Odd Girl Out: The hidden culture of aggression in girls* (Harcourt, 2002)

Emily White, *Fast Girls: Teenage tribes and the myth of the slut* (Scribner's, 2002)

Rosalind Wiseman, *Queen Bees & Wannabees: Helping your daughter survive cliques, gossip, boyfriends, and other realities of adolescence* (Crown, 2002)

Sharon Lamb, *The Secret Lives of Girls: The real feelings of young girls on sex, violence, and morality* (The Free Press, 2002)

Phyllis Chesler, *Woman's Inhumanity to Woman* (Thunder's Mouth Press/Nation Books, 2001)

Shelley Taylor, *The Tending Instinct: How nurturing is essential for who we are and how we live* (Henry Holt, 2002)

Carol Gilligan, *The Birth of Pleasure* (Knopf, 2002)

Man, it is *so* hard to live down that sugar-and-spice rep. We women try, Lord do we try, and still people are shocked—shocked!—when we are mean to each other, humiliate our partners, scream at our children, spread nasty rumors, lie on our résumés, embezzle from our employers, demean our employees, give slower drivers the finger, have extramarital affairs, commit murder, enter the military, join the Aryan Nation or the Islamic Jihad, and fail to send Christmas cards to the family. How dare women behave like . . . like . . . *people*?

In recent years, journalists, academics, and psychologists alike have been discovering that girls and women can be as aggressive and mean

The Chronicle of Higher Education, Review, B7-B9, July 5, 2002.

as men. Margaret Talbot's report in *The New York Times Magazine*, "Girls Just Want to be Mean," kicked things off. Rachel Simmons weighed in with *Odd Girl Out*, on the "hidden" culture of girls' aggression. It quickly became a *New York Times* bestseller. Rosalind Wiseman contributed *Queen Bees and Wannabees*, which offers parents advice on how to help their teenage daughters "survive cliques, gossip, boyfriends, and other realities of adolescence." Sharon Lamb, a clinical psychologist, wrote *The Secret Lives of Girls*, describing the fact that girls have sexual feelings, get angry, and can behave aggressively. Emily White focuses on *Fast Girls*, and how the "slut" is selected, slandered, and then cruelly ostracized by the adolescent in-groups that fear and envy her. And psychologist Phyllis Chesler reminds us that man's malevolence toward man isn't a patch on *Woman's Inhumanity to Woman*.

Naturally, the media have been salivating. Oprah, Dateline, and countless magazines have duly reported the news about all this hidden and formerly secret female aggressiveness, even though none of it seems to be terribly hidden or secret to women, or for that matter to men. To be fair, *Newsweek* balanced its report on the epidemic of mean girls with another cover story on the prevalence of non-mean girls.

Of course, gender differences are eternally fascinating, a source of amusement, anger, and exasperation; trying to understand one's own and the other sex is a popular indoor sport. But why aren't gender topics such as female aggressiveness evenly distributed, like raisins in a cake? Why do they bunch up, like buses on Fifth Avenue? You wait forever, and suddenly there's a cluster of them.

One reason is that trade publishers crave news; you must have something different to say, at least semi-shocking, to warrant publication. In the world of gender books, therefore, old news about female inequality won't do, such as those pesky world problems of discrimination, poverty, illiteracy, birth control, genital mutilation, and rape. Old news about female superiority won't do, either. The feel-good genre of the 1980s and 1990s—with its notion that women are kinder, better at friendship, and more moral, compassionate, earth-loving, and nurturant than men—is toast. And so the time and economy were just right for the new, not-new news that girls aren't sweeter than boys, but just as bad, sexual, and aggressive. Maybe girls are even meaner, given the ruthless and sneaky ways they control each other's sexuality, reputations, and impulses toward independence.

"Which sex is in trouble" books have another economic function: They drive public attention to social problems and help determine what resources will be directed to them. That is why, the national conversation is so often framed in terms of who is worse off. Who is having more trouble in schools: girls, who are more likely to be overlooked, or boys, who have more learning disabilities? Who has the greater self-esteem problem: girls, who feel insecure and fall silent, or boys, who feel insecure and brag? Who has the greater bullying problem: girls, who do it verbally, or boys,

45

who do it physically? Who has the eating and body-image disorders: white middle-class girls, with their familiar problems of anorexia and bulimia, or teenage boys, many of whom are taking dangerous amounts of steroids and pumping themselves up to meet a cultural ideal no less damaging than gauntness is for girls? How about African-American and Hispanic teenagers, of either sex, among whom rates of obesity are rising sharply?

Unquestionably, many aspects of our culture foster aggression, competition, and selfishness, and girls and women are hardly immune from those influences. Readers of *Woman's Inhumanity to Woman* will nod their heads and say, Chesler is so right. Many women do brutally control other women's sexuality by, for example, slandering, shaming, and excluding those who have "illicit" sex, and by perpetrating such brutal practices as female genital mutilation in Africa and other parts of the world. Many mothers are cold or neglectful; belittle their daughters if they are not pretty or thin enough; and try to assure their daughters' conformity. Although Chesler brings in studies and clinical material to support her case, her bitter tone and the personal experiences she reveals make one think her title could have been *Woman's Inhumanity to Me.*

Readers of health psychologist Shelley E. Taylor's *The Tending Instinct* will also nod their heads, saying that Taylor is right, too. Women's caretaking of their families, friends, parents, and neighbors makes social life possible. Throughout their lives, women love and rely on their friends. "Women and children have literally stayed alive over the centuries because women form friendships," writes Taylor. It's unattached males—packs of adolescent primates or lonely single adults—who get into trouble and cause trouble, and whose health plummets without the loving ministrations of a nurturing female. Taylor's optimistic, cheerful tone makes one think her title could have been *My Marvelous Female Friends.*

All this yinning and yanging about which sex is better or worse, which sex has the more pressing problems, would be funny if it were not so depressing for anyone who has studied or lived through enough swings of the pendulum. Menstruation makes women crazy and irrational? No, it makes women closer to the rhythms of the earth. Wait, no, it gives them PMS, which makes them crazy and irrational. Women are manipulative and cunning, competing with each other for men? No, they are the souls of peace and cooperative sisterhood. Wait, no, they are just as warlike as men.

Good old-fashioned American historical amnesia makes the eternal dilemmas of gender seem fresh in every incarnation, yet each generation also confronts problems specific to its era. Mean-girl books have struck pay dirt because they hit a nerve in the national parental psyche. Middle-class parents have become obsessed by the need to micromanage every aspect of their children's lives, starting with the pattern chosen for an infant's crib bumper to stimulate the baby's visual system. But it's one thing to try to control a baby's synapses, and quite another to try to control a teenager's. Many adults today are frightened *for* their teenagers, worrying about the real and imagined dangers of sex, STDs, the Internet, drugs, and violence; but also frightened *of* their teenagers—of their moodiness, unpredictability, potential for aggression.

Still, as Emily White observes in *Fast Girls*, "People have been afraid of teenagers for a long time." Teenagers disrupt the home, the order of things. They are awakening to sex, evoking worry and envy in their parents. Unencumbered as they are by the obligations of adulthood, they have an unquenchable longing for the rush of danger and risk. Some parental worries are, therefore, appropriate. But in today's anxious times worry is easily blown out of proportion by media scare stories. It's not enough to be frightened of teenage males, those troubled, violent "teenage time bombs" that *Time* warned us about; now we must fear girls, too.

In fact, the worry is way out of proportion to reality. The rate of violent crimes committed by adolescents has been plummeting steadily in the last decade, according to reports from the Federal Bureau of Investigation, and studies of representative samples of adolescents find that only a small minority are seriously troubled, angry, or unhappy. Many do suffer from peer pressure and exclusion, but extreme turmoil and unhappiness are the exception, not the rule. What problems are more common during adolescence? Conflict with parents, mood swings, and depression, the familiar pain of peer rejection and comparison, and higher rates of reckless, rule-breaking, and risky behavior. Not newsy enough for Oprah.

Neither is it news that males and females, being human, share in equal measure all the attributes of humanity, its graces and furies. Neither sex, in adolescence or any other time of life, has the corner on misery. Both are equally likely to be empathic, kind, altruistic, and friendly and to be mean, hostile, aggressive, petty, conformist, and prejudiced. Both sexes can be competitive or cooperative, selfish or nurturant, and reveal all of those qualities on different occasions.

However, books about gender similarities do not sell. Taylor told me that *The Tending Instinct* was originally called *Vital Ties*, and it was meant to be about the biology and social psychology of the human need for relationships, with some attention to gender differences but by no means the whole focus. Her publisher prevailed upon her to highlight the differences and to give the book its current title, although she is well aware, as she notes in the preface, that "'instinct' is a loaded word" (as in "maternal instinct") that has been discredited.

Of course the sexes often do differ, on the average, in how they express certain universal human qualities, and those are the differences that cause all the mischief and command our attention. For example, Taylor shows how nurturing is often expressed differently in men and women: Men are more likely to be heroic and altruistic by leaping into frozen rivers and burning buildings to rescue strangers; women, by sacrificing their own needs and time to care for aged parents and others in need of routine help. Both kinds of acts are selfless; both assure the survival of individuals and communities. A "tending society" makes sure that both are encouraged and rewarded, whichever sex is doing them.

Today, most books on gender are themselves gendered: not only directed to women, but also written in the feminized, personal, and elusive language of popular psychology. Whether the authors are academics or journalists, many of the books tend to share a similar level, tone, and formula: a combination of references to studies, informal interviews, lots and lots of anecdotes, and advice. There is nothing inherently wrong with this formula; the resulting book can still be interesting and useful. Indeed, I endorsed Lamb's book because, in an era when abstinence is the primary message of sex education, and when so many adults are quite irrational about the sexual feelings of children and teenagers, I liked its spirited message that girls, too, are sexual beings—as well as occasionally angry and aggressive beings who can learn to stand up for their rights.

But the gender-genre books that are based largely on clinical intuition and popular psychology typically lack a basic skepticism toward received wisdom. Thus, an hour after, I read Carol Gilligan's *The Birth of Pleasure*, I was hungry for a good idea. I haven't the foggiest notion what that book is about, but thousands of women will adore its soft flatteries that remind them of how they, too, were once free-spirited preteens with "authentic" voices and bold ambitions before life, patriarchy, and mean mothers crushed them. "I was drawn by the sound of an unmediated voice, a voice that broke free," Gilligan writes. "As I came back to a knowing I had learned to distance myself from or discredit, I saw girls beginning not to know what they knew." But maybe girls are also beginning to know what they didn't know. That used to be called growing up.

The typical gender-problem book starts like this: "As a girl (young woman/middle-aged woman/married woman/single woman/lesbian woman), I suffered horribly from X, Y, Z problem. I thought I was the only one. But then I talked to some other women and learned I wasn't alone! In fact, my problem was epidemic! That was so liberating!" Thus Simmons writes of her discovery that girls can be bullies: "It was exhilarating to discover we'd all been through the same ordeal. Like me, my friends had spent years believing they were the only ones." That is the fundamental sentence of all female-discovery books. It doesn't matter what the "ordeal" is: They masturbated, were gay, had an eating problem, had recovered a memory of being a French princess in a previous life. The discovery, of course, must be about something heretofore hidden. "Silence," says Simmons, "is deeply woven into the fabric of the female experience." Pardon? Putting "silence" in the same sentence with "female experience" is like putting cheese in fudge. It doesn't go.

Once the epiphany (and book contract) are attained, the writer sets out to find confirming cases of her hypothesis. She will usually cite supporting articles and throw around some numbers, but those don't mean much. As Simmons acknowledges, "This book is not the product of a formal research experiment. In it you will not find statistics or scientific conclusions about girls and aggression or information about boys." Or as Chesler describes her method: "Over the years, I have interviewed more than 500 women of all ages, classes, races, sexual persuasions, religions, and professions about this subject. I have also reviewed hundreds, possibly thousands of studies that bear on the subject." That kind of thing conveys an aura of reliability, but what does it mean? What kind of interviews, systematic or informal? How many ages, classes, religions? Did the answers vary by religion or profession? "Hundreds, possibly thousands" of studies? Well, which? Were they all equally good? What is the point of this accretion of numbers?

Again, a book does not have to be based on scientific evidence to be useful or enlightening. Scientific methods are crucial, however, if we want to know the actual prevalence of a problem, if we are willing to have our hypotheses disconfirmed, if we want to know whether and how the sexes differ, if we want to understand why a given social problem has arisen. Anecdote-driven accounts draw attention to a problem, but they fail to give us the big picture or an accurate one. Such books are dandelions: They look pretty and seem to cohere, but when you blow on their argument, it disappears.

For example, Simmons starts right out with a claim, "There is a hidden culture of girls' aggression in which bullying is epidemic, distinc-

tive, and destructive." She explains, "Our culture refuses girls access to open conflict, and it forces their aggression into nonphysical, indirect, and covert forms. Girls use backbiting, exclusion, rumors, name-calling, and manipulation to inflict psychological pain on targeted victims." Boys, in short, resort to physical aggression; girls to relational aggression.

That is true, but it is not the full truth or even the most interesting truth. For one thing, although physical aggression among girls and women is not anywhere as common or as dangerous as male violence, it is far from rare or hidden; neither are direct expressions of anger, as these authors' own interviewees often tell them. Conversely, suppressed or misdirected anger is common among boys and men. As for the lack of male relational aggression, does Simmons think that boys do not resort to *name-calling*? Boys have always had an array of offensive names: racist slurs, homophobic aspersions, cruel names for boys who are fat, slow, or "too smart." Boys do not exclude other boys of different ethnicities, or who are not as "masculine," cool, straight, athletic? Boys and men do not humiliate or "inflict psychological pain" on their victims? Boys and men do not have cliques that exclude outsiders?

In contrast, as a rare example of a book of astute insights with no pretense to science, White's *Fast Girls* leads the pack for its intelligent, original reportage. Its observations are refreshingly free of cant, sentiment, soupy psychology, and hypocrisy about teenage sexuality. The book is a meditation about the "slut," the word and its victims, drawn from a mix of memories, interviews with students, and diverse, unusual readings from theology to sociology. I found the observations original and charming: "Like a tribe in an ancient forest telling stories about the moon," White writes, "kids tell slut stories because they need an allegory for the mystery of sex itself."

The "slut story," far from reflecting what parents imagine to be the hypersexuality of teenaged girls, results in part from girls' sexual ignorance and inexperience. The media images of sexuality that girls are exposed to are sensational, prurient, and romantic, but not literally about sexual activities. White reports that "girls do not tend to have graphic conversations about sex the way boys do; they speak in terms of *Did you... ? Did you... ?* Thus the slut and her rumored acts exist in an elliptical darkness; her techniques are a mystery. Faced with this mystery and with no way to alleviate it, girls lash out.... Girls hate the slut because she is a story they are not allowed in on."

The books on gender and feminism that exploded onto the cultural landscape in the 1960s and 1970s took on many of the same subjects as today's crop does, including female insecurity, backbiting, competition for men, anger, silence, sexual ignorance, and nurturance. But there is a big difference: In most of today's books, the politics and passion, the courage and anger, the analysis of the impact of culture and context on behavior, have been stripped away, leaving the solipsism of one's own experience: "My troubles with my bitchy female boss" means "all female bosses are bitchy." In the 1970s, social scientists like Rosabeth Moss Kanter (in *Men and Women of the Corporation*) showed that bitchiness was not a matter of gender, but of position in the organizational hierarchy: Bosses of either sex who have little real authority and low chances of promotion are more likely to take it out on their employees. Similarly, both sexes are more inclined to express hostility and aggression directly to those with less power than they; when they perceive no consequences to their actions; or when they feel anonymous (hence all those belligerent female drivers of SUVs). Today, bitchy behavior or aggressiveness is regarded as inflexible personality traits, inherent in a person's gender by virtue of hormones, socialization, or genetics.

Accordingly, in the spirit of the day, Wiseman, Lamb, and Simmons dispense psychological advice: how to understand your teen's behavior, how to talk to her, and how not to talk to her. (Only Emily White, again to her eternal credit, allows readers to draw their own conclusions about what, if anything, to do.) There is nothing wrong with good advice, and parents may find useful suggestions in these books. Yet it is also important to think about what it would take to create a "tending society" and make schools more appealing, more cooperative places to attend. The psychologizing of social problems is so much easier, because psychology directs us to look inward, to personal solutions rather than institutional changes. People cannot control the fact that peers are powerfully important to adolescents, and parents cannot force a child to fit in to an unwelcoming group. But they can supervise and influence the kind of peer groups their child belongs to, help the child find groups in which he or she will thrive, and press for programs that foster cooperation rather than competition among groups.

In the same spirit, as long as we keep seeing the sexes as opposite players in some unwinnable zero-sum game, rather than as allies seeking to solve a specific problem, *whoever* suffers from it, society's responses will careen drunkenly from one sex to the other, depending on who is making the most noise, whose problem seems worse, and whose problem makes the news this week. And as long as women focus exclusively inward to their feelings and their pasts, they will lack the knowledge and will to find solutions beyond the self, to think about how to reframe the conversation away from "us versus them" and forward to "us and them."

PART III

PSYCHOTHERAPY AND THE SCIENTIST-PRACTITIONER GAP

11

■ ■ ■

The Body Never Lies
The Lingering Effects of Hurtful Parenting

By Alice Miller

The narcissism at the core of Alice Miller's writing and the impoverished quality of her scholarship are evident in her notes. The Introduction has four notes, three of them to her own previous works. Chapter 2 has two notes, one of them to an earlier book of hers. Chapter 9 has only one note, to one of her books. Chapter 11 has no notes, but it begins by describing the fear the author felt when she was writing *Thou Shalt Not Be Aware.* Chapter 12, a brief essay about a French serial killer who, she claims, murdered his victims because of his repressed hatred of his mother, has two notes, one to one of her books and the other to a profile of the killer in *Le Monde,* which appears to be the sole source of Miller's analysis of his life. Nine chapters have no notes at all. In spite of Miller's repeated claims that her ideas are based on empirical evidence as well as observations in psychotherapy, she provides only one note to anything faintly like a research study, and it is not even to a published study in a peer-reviewed journal, but rather to a summary of the study on a website.

Alice Miller, who died in 2010 at the age of 87, wrote the same book over and over for years, and its theme is simple: It is time to get rid of the Fourth Commandment to honor thy father and thy mother. If thy father and thy mother have been abusive, neglectful, violent, or cruel, they do not deserve honoring. In fact, they do not deserve your empathy, compassion, or forgiveness, unless they beg your forgiveness first. Certainly, this is a moral matter that deserves debate, but ultimately it is a personal decision.

Times Literary Supplement, October 27, 2006.

Neither science nor psychology can provide an inherently correct answer that applies to everyone, but Miller believes that she can.

Miller's theory was that uncritical parent-honoring "frequently prevents us from admitting our true feelings, and that we pay for this compromise with various forms of illness"; she claimed that her book "contains many examples that substantiate this theory," as if examples were scientific evidence. If we are going to argue from personal experience, then all of us can indeed provide examples of people who were better off when they severed relations with "toxic" parents. But most of us can also provide counter-examples of people who, by trying to understand the genetic, cultural, and historical reasons for their parents' failures and cruelties, were able to acknowledge the good things their parents did for them, let go of anger about the bad things, and accept the fact that they were never going to transform their mother or father into the loving, supportive parent they longed for.

Needless to say, it is not easy to do this. A friend explained why she was continuing to care for her elderly mother, who would have won the gold if there were an awful-parent Olympics. My friend was able to forgive her mother, she said, by understanding that the pain the mother suffers because of her neuroses is far worse than any pain she inflicted on her daughter. My friend learned not to take her mother's actions personally, but to see the anguish behind the anger and venom and to be grateful for the good things her mother did for her.

Miller would have none of this forgiveness business. She brooked no compromises, either, as in "focus on the good your parents did and forgive the bad"—attitudes that she regards as denial, repression of true feelings, and a betrayal of a small child's entitlement to total, unconditional love. Her position stemmed from her own unwillingness or inability to forgive her parents for the cruelties they inflicted on her for being an unwanted girl instead of the hoped-for boy. "Only when I allowed myself to feel the emotions pent up in me for so long inside me did I start extricating myself from my own past," she wrote "I cannot force myself to love or honor my parents if my body rebels against such an endeavor for reasons that are well-known to it. . . . My aim was to be loved as a daughter. But the effort was all in vain." It took Miller 48 years "to discover the need to paint and to allow myself to gratify that need," and it took her even longer to "concede myself the right not to love my parents."

Even if adult children consciously try to forgive their parents, Miller asserts, their bodies will not allow them to: Repressed anger will make itself felt in bodily symptoms ranging from migraines to obesity. Hence, "the body never lies." (Of course it lies. It lies all the time, as when it deceives us that all is well while plotting to give us arthritis or cancer.) It is a shame that Miller never bothered to investigate the interesting research on the physiological as well as psychological benefits of forgiveness, of setting down the burden of grudges and grievances.

Alice Miller became hugely popular in the early 1980s, with her book

Prisoners of Childhood (soon retitled to the more reader-flattering *The Drama of the Gifted Child*), and it quickly became one of the bibles of the parent-blaming, recovered-memory culture of victimization. Are you fat, do you have headaches, do you have intestinal difficulties, are you unmotivated, do you smoke too much? Has it taken you nearly 50 years to get out your paintbrushes? Poor child, you were not loved enough; you were too gifted, brilliant . . . unappreciated. You can't remember being abused? Your body does.

In *The Body Never Lies,* Miller never paused long enough to define what, precisely, she is talking about, let alone to bolster her argument with anything as tedious as scientific data. Readers who love her will cry in recognition of her case studies (which suspiciously conform to her argument and sound awfully like her own voice). The rest of us will cry, too, but in exasperation. Sometimes 'abuse' means violent beatings or incest, but sometimes it includes routine spankings; sometimes it is physical, sometimes psychological; sometimes it is squashing a child's spirit, but sometimes it is simply putting limits on what the child wants to do; sometimes it is rejecting and neglecting a child, but sometimes it is failing to read a child's mind and knowing the child is unhappy. Whatever form it takes, "abuse" is responsible, Miller claimed, for all the ills of the body and the world—anorexia, neurodermatitis, serial killers, and power-mad dictators. It shortens its victims' lives, except for those who live to a ripe old age, in which case it lessens the quality of their lives.

In the 25 years since Miller's first book, there has been an explosion of research in behavioral genetics, child development, emotions, memory, eating disorders, children's resilience, stress-induced disorders, the nonfalsifiable premises of psychoanalytic theory, and the confirmation bias—the tendency we all have to seek out only that information which confirms what we already believe. Miller's confirmation bias was narrower than most, being almost entirely self-referential. A physician who was still promoting medical beliefs and interventions that had been discredited decades earlier would be out of business. There was no excuse for what seems a willful blindness to the advances of science in her own profession, especially one that has such direct impact on her devoted readers' lives, but obviously there is. She was an abused child.

12

■ ■ ■

Into the Minds of Madmen

How the FBI's Behavioral Science Unit Revolutionized Crime Investigation

By Don DeNevi and John H. Campbell

This is a dull and trivial book about a vitally important subject: the effort to make crime detection more scientific. The FBI set up its Behavioral Science Unit (BSU) in 1972, and promptly produced a new psycho-detective tool called the "criminal profile." Criminal profiling made the BSU famous among police officers, novelists, and filmmakers. "When local police are stumped and stymied, when they have little hope of tracking down the demons, they turn to the FBI's legendary Behavioral Science Unit," Don DeNevi writes in his typically breathless prose. "The BSU stalks [these human-killers], down the paths of their own minds."

DeNevi went to the FBI academy intending to "write the history of the BSU for the people of America." DeNevi is something of a professional cheerleader for the FBI, but even his own track record of writing books characterized by uncritical devotion to the academy was not enough to win him the cooperation of the BSU, whose men (only men) he wanted to glorify in this volume. So DeNevi enlisted as his co-author John Campbell, a former unit chief of the BSU and academic dean of the FBI academy. Doors opened; people told DeNevi

Times Literary Supplement, August 20, 2004.

that Campbell gave the project "the stamp of the imprimatur. Suddenly, you and the project are credible."

Credible to them, perhaps; to the rest of us, the book is as incredible as a government propaganda report. Interviewees speak like this: "Yes, we often felt sick to our stomachs [about the nasty crimes they were called upon to solve]. But we had a job to do. We were to offer support to law enforcement that couldn't do the job. After us, there was no one. If we didn't help solve the case, who would?" DeNevi describes everyone with glowing praise—[BSU chief Roger Depue] "was the consummate leader, handling everyone with dignity"—and, in his account, everyone gets along with everyone else in a collegial spirit of affection and respect. The braying of a sole ego never rises above the hum of teamwork.

DeNevi wants to impress us with the BSU's practice of developing investigative methods derived from rigorous, empirically validated research. Of these methods, the most famous became criminal profiling—noting patterns across crimes, inferring certain likely qualities of a criminal from details found at a crime scene. Profiling has on occasion been helpful to detectives, particularly when it derives from objective actuarial information, but it is also supremely vulnerable to investigator bias and pseudoscientific mumbojumbo. Readers will learn nothing here of the limitations and controversies surrounding the practice of profiling, whose practitioners apparently are never in doubt and never wrong.

A profiler with shortcomings? Not in DeNevi's world. A chapter on nine of the founding members of the BSU begins: "We asked, during a recent interview, 'You mean, then, the Nine were able to combine body, mind, and spirit to solve the most difficult of crimes?' The answer was an unequivocal, 'Yes'." The conceit behind that unequivocal "yes" is precisely the problem with many profilers.

Yet the alert reader may detect, between the lines of DeNevi's glowing stories of his heroes and their alleged successes, some of the inherent problems with profiling. For example, Jack Kirsch, a former chief of the BSU, tells DeNevi that visiting police officers would come up to his team members with difficult cases and ask for advice. "As impromptu as it was, we weren't afraid to shoot from the hip and we usually hit our targets. We did this thousands of times." This cowboy confidence is born of a training that rewards speed and certainty over caution and doubt. Members of the BSU, like psychiatrists and clinicians, learn to make quick judgments and to be convinced of their accuracy. Unfortunately, this training often fosters an arrogance that blinds practitioners to the possibility of error. And it is utterly inimical to the training of true scientists, taught to value uncertainty, to consider many possible explanations before choosing a likely one, and, most important, to find ways of counteracting the confirmation bias—the human tendency to ignore or discount evidence that is discrepant with one's beliefs or, in detective work, one's initial hunches.

Practitioners of profiling learn to notice the hits—the bits of evidence across cases that seem to indicate a

59

criminal's pattern—and to overlook or trivialize evidence that does not fit the pattern. David Cole, in his book *No Equal Justice,* listed the profiles of alleged drug couriers that had justified the arrests of suspects in American airports: the person traveled alone or traveled with a companion; arrived late at night, early in the morning, or in the afternoon; carried a small bag, a medium-sized bag, two bulky garment bags, or four pieces of luggage; was one of first to deplane, the last to deplane, or deplaned in the middle. . . . In short, once an investigator or police officer regards someone as a suspect, anything that person does confirms the suspicion.

In other cases, profilers often produce a prediction that is fuzzy and obvious, although they usually speak in such authoritative tones that they quell any skeptics. One famous profiler, James Reese, told DeNevi of being called on to offer a profile of a murder suspect who was trapped in a forest, surrounded by 40 heavily armed police officers. The suspect had killed the housekeeping manager of his motel, apparently because she entered his room unexpectedly. He escaped through a window and fled into the woods, leaving a diary behind indicating that he was one angry Vietnam vet. "While not qualified to diagnose," Reese said, "and in the BSU we are not allowed to label people" (he then, of course, proceeds to diagnose and label the suspect), "I believe him to be paranoid schizophrenic based upon his behavior in the motel room and his writings found in the diary, which are full of racial terms like 'gook,' 'chink,' 'yellow bastard,' 'Charlie,'

etc." (Reese fails to note that these dehumanizing terms for the enemy are common among soldiers who are not paranoid schizophrenics.)

Reese then predicts that the suspect is a discharged Marine and "when you capture him, you'll find he has dug four or five foxholes out there in the trees, plus he has plenty of ammunition for his rifle, and is in full Marine Corps gear." He advises the police not to go in at night with helicopters because the suspect would undoubtedly fire at them. Keep the guy awake until morning, he advises, when he will be easier to capture or shoot. The police are dazzled by Reese's prognostication. But is it anything other than the obvious?

The BSU was from its inception vulnerable to pseudoscience, particularly the psychoanalytic habit of confusing labels with explanations. The labels don't actually help the police catch anyone; after all, little is gained by knowing that some mad killer is probably a paranoid loner who hates his mother. But *once the suspect is caught, his behavior can be made to fit the profile,* counting as a success for the profiler. One of the early practitioners of profiling, psychiatrist James A. Brussel, claimed he could diagnose an unknown offender's mental disorder from evidence at the crime scene. He decided that George Metesky, the Mad Bomber who terrorized New York in the 1950s, was a "paranoic." "Unconsciously, Metesky fashioned his bombs like penises because of unresolved psychosexual issues when he was a little boy," Brussel wrote in a book about his cases. "The W's in his letters always have rounded bottoms, suggesting women's breasts." (At least that's what they suggested to Brussel.) Brussel predicted that the Mad Bomber would never respond to psychiatric treatment, that psychoanalysis "would wash over him like water off a duck's back," and that when he was finally imprisoned he would be a model citizen. Even today, BSU profilers say that such behavior is characteristic of all serial bombers. But it is also characteristic of psychopaths, rapists, wife abusers, embezzlers, gangsters, corrupt corporate officials, and countless others.

Brussel's profile of the Mad Bomber also had some accurate descriptors, but his erroneous profile of the Boston Strangler in 1964 led the police on a wild goose chase. Profilers, however, are rarely fazed by error. Like psychics and astrologers whose predictions fail, they explain away mistakes as flukes, and thus feel no need to change the assumptions on which their predictions are made. Psychics, astrologers, and palm readers all count on people's willingness to think that a generic personality profile, one vague enough to apply to just about anybody ("sometimes you feel insecure"), describes them *exactly.* Many profilers, too, fail to see how many elements of their profiles simply reflect the baseline rates of a particular behavior in the general population or among a category of offender. One profiler noted that all the victims of a serial rapist-murderer were women (surprise!) and that the offender chose remote sites on which to dispose of his victims (where else would he leave them, a department store?), except of course for the times he chose public sites, such as the side of the road. The profiler predicted that the offender would have a prior history of violence, that his favorite colors would be black, dark blue, and brown (the commonest colors that men choose), and that he would probably be single—all obvious inferences from the statistics on violent men.

The use of statistics in narrowing the field of possible suspects, and of objective crime-scene evidence in determining the criminal's *modus operandi,* are clearly essential in crime detection. But in tracking down the "madmen" of this book's title, many profilers continue in the obsolete clinical tradition characterized by psychiatric labeling and the confirmation bias.

My favorite story from this book was the BSU's effort to identify the Unabomber who terrorized America some years ago by sending complex bombs in letters and parcels to selected targets in the world of high technology. The BSU's profile was once again a masterpiece of the obvious: the bomber would be a "highly intelligent, deliberate, patient, imaginative, technically competent individual." The Unabomber then sent a manifesto, explaining his motives, to the *New York Times,* which published it. The BSU scrutinized the document and concluded that the Unabomber would prove to be "A white male, forty to fifty-five years of age who failed to achieve a postgraduate degree; who lived, worked, attended school, or made extensive visits to the Chicago area; who possibly attended trade school; and who was anger- or revenge-motivated." That certainly narrows the field! Would anyone care to estimate the number of people setting off bombs who are not anger- or revenge-motivated? The Unabomber was eventually caught, but only because his brother turned him in.

Because profilers get so much public attention, are usually portrayed on screen by someone dashing and brilliant, and have so much authority in courtroom testimony, it is regrettable that this book is such a puff piece. Until the FBI's Behavioral Science Unit truly gets the science part into its practice, they are merely doing science fiction.

13

■ ■ ■

Remembering Trauma

By Richard J. McNally

Out of the Dark

By Linda Caine and Robin Royston

One of these books is the prob-lem; the other, the solution. No two works could more clearly illuminate the issues in the bitter fight over the nature of memory and trauma that has been waged for more than two decades in America and Britain. It has not been the usual academic dispute, where opponents accuse one another of woeful ignorance and disgraceful slop-piness and then adjourn to the nearest pub. The memory wars, like all wars, involve face-saving, livelihoods, repu-tations, and politics. No other dispute in psychology and psychiatry touches people so passionately, because we *are* our memories.

The dispute concerns an array of beliefs and practices promulgated largely by psychotherapists, including psychiatrists, clinical psychologists, and social workers. In their view, the mind tries to protect itself from the horrors of traumatic experiences ei-ther through "repression," the mecha-nism that allegedly prevents threatening memories from reaching conscious-ness, or through "dissociation," a dis-ruption in consciousness in which the bad memory splits off and the victim suffers amnesia for the disturbing event. Many therapists further assume that sexual abuse occupies its own special category of horror, a trauma worse than being imprisoned in a con-centration camp or witnessing the murder of a parent. For those who take this view, it is not only possible,

Times Literary Supplement, August 15, 2003.

but common, for a woman to be sexually molested and even raped by her father, sometimes for years, only to repress the memory until it is recovered in therapy.

These beliefs, widely held today, actually developed only after 1980. Before that, clinicians who were treating survivors of war, torture, incest, and other ordeals observed that clients were reluctant to talk about their experiences, but all remembered them. No Holocaust survivor had repressed the horrors of the camps. Yet by the end of the 1980s, as Richard J. McNally writes, "reluctance to disclose became inability to remember." The appropriate therapy for uprooting the buried memory involved dream analysis, hypnosis, interpreting bodily symptoms as evidence of past trauma, and similar suggestive techniques. For the thousands of people who do not forget traumatic experiences, help arrived for them, too. In 1980, the American Psychiatric Association gave its imprimatur to the diagnosis of Posttraumatic Stress Disorder (PTSD), and by the end of the decade the trauma industry was in full swing. In the aftermath of any disaster, natural or human-made, swarms of therapists appear on the scene to help victims recover and head off PTSD at the pass. Trauma therapy is a growth industry around the world.

The beliefs concerning recovered memory and the treatment of trauma are the latest in a long line of psychological ideas and diagnoses that have gained ascendancy in the clinical world and popular culture before collapsing under the weight of scientific evidence—such as phrenology, mesmerism, penis envy, Munchausen by Proxy Syndrome, and multiple personality disorder. The losing factions have not yielded gracefully. They are reacting as, I imagine, phrenologists must have done in the twilight of phrenology, as evidence accumulated that one cannot identify a thief by the "stealing bumps" on his head: by dismissing the data and doubling their fee.

McNally, a professor of psychology at Harvard University, is both a clinician who studies anxiety disorders and one of the leading scientific investigators in the field of trauma and memory. *Remembering Trauma* is an exhaustive review of the scientific research and clinical evidence pertaining to trauma and memory, including what is known about dreams and nightmares, flashbacks, repression, dissociation, amnesia, and posttraumatic stress disorder. No relevant question escapes his scrutiny: Are nightmares literal memories? What is repression, exactly, and how does it differ from normal forgetting? What is a trauma, exactly, and why do some people continue to have emotional symptoms when most recover? McNally resists the conciliatory impulse to take a middle ground, perhaps along the lines of "recovered memories occur more often than some people think but less than others think." Nonsense, he says. Some people think the world is round and others may say it is flat, but "neither science nor reason requires us to conclude that the world is therefore oblong."

There are no oblong compromises in *Remembering Trauma,* only the most scrupulous conclusions based on what the evidence shows, or fails to show. "The notion that the mind protects itself by repressing or dissociating memories of trauma, rendering them inaccessible to awareness," McNally summarizes, "is a piece of psychiatric folklore devoid of convincing empirical support." So, surprisingly, is the belief in the widespread occurrence of psychogenic amnesia, in which a person cannot remember key events because they are psychologically shocking. This phenomenon is as beloved by novelists and filmmakers as by clinicians, but it is extremely rare. Most cases of amnesia in the aftermath of trauma or accident are organic, caused by damage to the brain.

McNally's goal is to explain and persuade, which he does with a dazzling accumulation of evidence from a vast array of sources: laboratory research, physiological studies of the brain, clinical case studies, and studies of survivors of war, torture, rape, incest, sniper attacks, and other horrific experiences. The problem for survivors is not repressing their memories; it is that they have trouble forgetting them. People may not think about disturbing events or talk about them for long periods of time and then recall them later, but there is no reason, McNally observes, to "postulate a special mechanism of repression or dissociation" to explain this.

Further, the remembrance of things past is always distorted; memory is neither a perfect recording of events that can be replayed at will nor a buried object that can be dug up whole, like a potato. All memories—of upsetting experiences or exhilarating ones, of sudden shocking events or happy mundane ones—are subject to modification and change over time. This is not welcome information to most of us, and certainly not to therapists who rely on their client's memories as the key to the client's problems. Therapists who regard a patient's dreams and nightmares as a royal road to the unconscious or as evidence of buried memories won't like McNally's review of this research, either. Nightmares, it turns out, are common in the general population and they are unrelated to any measures of anxiety or psychopathology. Although many trauma survivors complain of having frequent nightmares, they actually have them no more often than anyone else.

Especially damning for the claims of the trauma industry, research shows that most survivors of trauma eventually overcome their normal emotional distress, especially if they can avoid the well-meaning interventions of trauma counselors. Of course, some survivors do continue to have extreme emotional symptoms years after a trauma, but the reasons seem to have less to do with the nature of the trauma itself than with their own preexisting traits, genetic predispositions, brain anomalies, and psychological resources. Thus, some people survive unspeakable horrors with no lasting PTSD symptoms, whereas others develop PTSD after non-life-threatening events, such as seeing "The Exorcist" or, as in one clinical case, after accidentally killing some frogs with a lawnmower.

Remembering Trauma is full of such surprising and illuminating findings, but it is not only about the mechanisms of memory and trauma. Its larger story is about the differences between scientists and clinicians in how they reason and the evidence they rely on to draw conclusions. Therapists tend to speak in grand generalizations; one wrote that children who experience repeated traumatic events "may forget whole segments of childhood—from birth to age 9, for example." Scientists cannot tolerate this vagueness. Their research finds that most of us forget "whole segments" of our childhoods and no one remembers anything from birth to age 2 or 3; such forgetting is perfectly normal and not evidence of trauma or repression. Likewise, the reader will come to share McNally's frustration with clinicians who refuse to yield a beloved concept even when they can't define it, measure it, or demonstrate it. When scientists take one definition of repression or dissociation and demolish it, the clinicians say, "well, we meant something else, and in any case we know it when we see it, and you don't."

If no one took it seriously, *Out of the Dark* would make an excellent companion to McNally's, for it perfectly illustrates every false assumption, cliché, and misunderstanding about the mind and memory that McNally demolishes. Reading these two books in tandem reveals the vast chasm between psychologists trained as scientists and those trained only to do therapy—the chasm that created the memory wars.

Linda Caine and her therapist, Robin Royston, alternate chapters in telling the story of Caine's therapy for depression and her "harrowing journey to discover her past." Royston was a physician, intending to specialize in anesthetics, until his wife gave him a book on dreams by Carl Jung. He immediately decided that he could best help people by becoming a Jungian analyst. Unfortunately, Jungian analysis is an approach that bypasses not only the entire field of clinical psychology, including the part about the utility (and failure) of different therapeutic methods, but also the entire field of scientific psychology, including the part showing that dreams are not memories nor evidence of anything that has actually happened. "We know so little about the human mind," says Royston, presumably using the royal we. "My knowledge of blocked memories comes from practical experience." This is precisely the problem.

Caine's life was a procession of tragedies, all of which she remembered perfectly: a mother who abandoned her as a child, an unnecessary mastectomy at age 14, a painful, self-inflicted abortion at 16, a violent husband whom she left, a rape by a potential employer. Remarried, she is nonetheless depressed and suicidal, and seeks therapy. It does not occur to her to wonder how many women with her history would not be depressed. Yet when Royston asks her what's wrong, she replies: "I don't know. I feel awful and I don't know why. . . . I think there is something evil in me'." Ah. Evil! Now we have a book! And so she and Royston start hunting down the Ultimate Memory, the great repressed event that must be the source of her current misery and suicidal impulses. We get countless dreams, because you cannot be in Jungian therapy without recounting the minutiae of your brain's normal nighttime sorties with horrid creatures. For hundreds of pages, with Caine's symptoms getting worse (as they typically do when patients spend years ruminating about their symptoms without getting proper treatment), she and Royston persist in trying to dig out the greatest horror.

It is a shame that Caine hadn't read *Remembering Trauma,* where she would have learned that her problem was depression, not repression. (Depressed people do often have impaired memories, McNally shows, not for the specific traumas of their lives, but for other autobiographical details.) Nonetheless, at last, the Ultimate Memory is uprooted: a vague impression that her mother, before leaving her family, had brought a man home to abuse Linda sexually while the mother watched. Even Caine finds this supposed memory improbable, and there is no way for her to corroborate the story, with her mother dead. "But it *has*

to be real," she writes. "It can't be my imagination." (Why not? Dream analysis is entirely about imagination.) "I wouldn't know about them and exactly how they would feel if I hadn't experienced them." (Of course she would; that's what it means to have an imagination, and in any case false memories feel as real as true ones.) "I buried it so deeply it only came up in nightmares." (Memories are not "buried" and nightmares are not evidence of memories anyway.) "If what I've written . . . is true, why don't I remember it as clearly as I do the other horrible things in my life?" (Because it probably isn't true.) "Why does it have a dreamlike, evasive quality?" (That is what pseudomemories are often like.)

The book has a happy ending: Caine terminates therapy and moves to California. But if there is to be a happy ending to the epidemic of psychological ignorance and therapeutic malpractice in the domains of memory and trauma, it is McNally's book that the public should read, and that every therapist must.

14

■ ■ ■

In Therapy We Trust
America's Obsession with
Self-Fulfillment

By Eva S. Moskowitz

America's obsession with therapy and self-fulfillment is a big, fat, sitting target that invites ridicule. It's so easy to take a thwack at all the self-help groups, goofy therapies, talk shows, and self-esteem-inflating programs that blot the American landscape. No wonder social critics have found the target irresistible.

Tom Wolfe started the modern ball rolling in 1973, with his brilliant essay, "The Me Decade." That decade produced R. D. Rosen's *Psychobabble*, the word and the book; Martin Gross's *The Psychological Society*, which assessed the burgeoning marketplace of therapies promoting self-fulfillment and human potential; and Christopher Lasch's classic *The Culture of Narcissism*. In the 1980s, Bernie Zilbergeld's *The Shrinking of America* skewered America's optimistically naïve beliefs that psychological change is not only possible but easy, that people should always be happy, and if they are not happy they need fixing.

In the 1990s, Philip Cushman's *Constructing the Self, Constructing America*, Ellen Herman's *The Romance of American Psychology*, and James Hillman and Michael Ventura's *We've Had a Hundred Years of Psychotherapy—And the World's Getting Worse* contributed their own distinctive analyses of the culturally popular belief that poverty, war, aging, and plumpness are all matters of failed will power and negative thinking. Robyn Dawes's *House of Cards: Psychology and psychotherapy built on myth* showed how many social programs and educa-

Times Literary Supplement, February 14, 2003.

tional policies in American culture, such as the self-esteem movement and abstinence-based drug and sex-education programs, are based on pseudoscience and subjective clinical opinion. They don't work, but they persist anyway because they reflect American cultural values or political agendas of the left and right.

The latest entrant from therapy critics is Eva Moskowitz, whose book *In Therapy We Trust* traces the origins and expansion of what she calls the "therapeutic gospel":

> We live in an age consumed by worship of the psyche. In a society plagued by divisions of race, class, and gender we are nonetheless bound together by a gospel of psychological happiness. Rich or poor, black or white, male or female, straight or gay, we share a belief that feelings are sacred and salvation lies in self-esteem, that happiness is the ultimate goal and psychological healing the means.

The "therapeutic gospel," Moskowitz argues, is more than a substitute religion; it permeates politics, education, business, and family life. "Psychological idolatry knows no bounds; it permeates everything, from the social-welfare system to the criminal-justice system. . . . Our therapeutic faith dictates that whatever the social problem, it can be solved psychologically." Thus, are inner city riots due to overcrowding, poverty, police abuse? The cure is not jobs, city services, and police reform, but an infusion of conflict-resolution programs. Are schoolchildren ignorant and illiter-ate? Bring in the motivational experts and the self-esteem programs.

Moskowitz believes that America's psychological idolatry sprung from the ideas of a mid-nineteenth century clockmaker named Phineas Quimby. Whereas the Victorians emphasized duty and self-denial, Quimby preached the importance of happiness, and his "mind healing" approach was designed to correct the "false ideas" that impeded people from achieving it. (Quimby hardly invented the American pursuit of happiness, which after all was one of the inalienable rights described in the Declaration of Independence one hundred years earlier.) Quimby's own approach was a forerunner of modern cognitive behavior therapy, though it was neither original with him nor particularly American. Epictetus and the Stoics had already told us that "it is not the things themselves that disturb men, but their judgments about these things."

Nonetheless, the hugely popular New Thought movement, in which Quimby played a major role, promoted "mind cures" to eradicate self-doubt, anxiety, shyness, melancholia, and other normal human miseries. In the twentieth century, according to Moskowitz, war, rapid social and economic changes, and industrialization led to the proliferation of mental-health experts, who made it their job to cure men of battle fatigue, couples of marital fatigue, juvenile delinquents and wives of disobedience, and political activists of rebelliousness.

Certainly Moskowitz is correct that many Americans sing in the choir of the therapeutic gospel. Unfortunately, this book is so ill-researched and poorly argued that even those sympathetic to her premise may come away exasperated. Moskowitz argues by assertion, not demonstration; her text is full of unreferenced claims and unattributed remarks that require the reader to search the endnotes to find the source. She lists a parade of therapies and counselors that she apparently regards as being equally silly, but some, such as rehabilitation counselors and behavior therapists, are helpful and effective; would she have us reject them all?

Similarly, she makes half-true claims, such as: "In the courtroom, psychological defenses multiply: the adopted-child syndrome, the battered-wife syndrome, the distant-father syndrome, the American Dream syndrome, and the Super Bowl Sunday syndrome." It's easy to mock the proclivity of American psychiatry to invent a new syndrome a week. But although defense attorneys keep trying to identify syndromes that might mitigate the severity of a defendant's sentence, they are rarely successful in court.

After a while, I found that Moskowitz's inflated and uncritical assertions were making me question her basic argument. Is America alone in its attraction to psychological explanations? Freud, who is conspicuously absent in this book, had, I dimly recall, something of an influence in Europe. Buenos Aires has the highest per capita number of psychoanalysts in the world; do the Argentines also qualify for therapeutic gospel credits? Are Americans the only ones addicted to talk-show pseudopsychology? These shows are hugely popular all over the world. How much of the American emphasis on feelings and self-improvement stems from distinctive aspects of American history and culture, and how much results from affluence, boredom, a glut of mental-health professionals creating new problems to treat, and an unregulated media eager to distract their audiences from political matters?

In Therapy We Trust sends many pointed darts into the heart of its sitting target, but it does not answer these questions. The target won't topple until we can.

15

■ ■ ■

Prisoners of Hate
The Cognitive Basis of
Anger, Hostility, and Violence

By Aaron T. Beck

The twentieth century began with the ascendancy of the unconscious and ended with the hegemony of the conscious. The cognitive revolution in psychology and neuroscience is transforming our vision of human behavior, moving us beyond the gloomy Freudian metaphors of mental processes and the mechanistic principles of behaviorism. We are, therefore we think. But what we think, how we think, and the power of our thoughts to influence our emotions and actions is the focus of new theories of the mind.

Though some would say it's our old mammalian brain that causes trouble, generating all those lovely but archaic urges for sex, food, and wine, it's actually our cerebral cortex that gets us into mischief and danger. If I insult my border collie to her face, she will not feel obliged to bite me. She will look at me adoringly and lick my hand. When she meets another dog, the two of them know exactly how to behave, without breaking the rules of dog decorum and, generally, without either harming the other. In contrast, human beings are the only species that can (and does) say, "The more I thought about it, the madder I got." Our mighty cortex, which gave us penicillin, poetry, and crossword puzzles, is also the source of bigotry, self-righteousness, and rationalization.

In *Prisoners of Hate,* Aaron T. Beck, a psychiatrist who was once a devout Freudian and went on to become one of the fathers of modern cognitive psychotherapy in America, turns his attention to the power of human cognition to generate anger, hostility, and violence. These plagues

Times Literary Supplement, December 17, 1999.

of existence, argues Beck, are not caused by inner furies or by testosterone-crazed males; rather, they are a result of normal cognitive processes. Thus, he maintains, if we can understand the mechanisms by which we think ourselves into anger and violence, we can think our way out of them.

Beck examines the "cognitive commonalities" involved in the thinking that underlies every form of anger and aggression, from "personal verbal abuse to prejudice and bigotry to war and genocide." When people feel threatened, frightened, or anxious, they revert to primal thinking: egocentric ("how dare this happen to *me*?"), dichotomous ("I'm good, you're evil"; "our nation is peaceful, theirs is brutal"), and stereotypic (all of "them" are cruel, lazy, stupid, or stingy). Primal thinking is "primal," according to Beck, in "the sense of being absolute—it occurs at the earliest stage of information processing—and also of being apparent in the early developmental phases, when children think largely in global evaluative terms, such as good or bad."

Certainly Beck is right that people who are quick to anger see the world differently from those who are slow to provocation. Angry people store grudges the way a squirrel stores acorns. They take things personally; they "mind read," assuming without evidence that another person's motives are malevolent; they feel unfairly treated. Violent individuals (and nations) also have characteristic beliefs that rationalize their behavior, for example, that violence is the only way to get respect, to restore their pride and honor, to maintain their status. They are incapable of empathy, of seeing a situation from any but an egocentric perspective.

Beck regards the hostile actions that result from primal thinking as "a strategy that was adaptive in early stages of our prehistory but is mainly maladaptive today." But aggression and hostility are not maladaptive. They persist precisely because they are so often successful: The bully gets the toy, the control over others, the power, the country.

Likewise, cognitive universals such as stereotyping, ethnocentrism, and us-them thinking are themselves neither good or bad; it's a sign of primal thinking to think that they are! They have many positive functions: stereotypes help us retrieve memories and make more efficient decisions. They allow us to organize experience, make sense of differences among individuals and groups, and predict how people will behave. Ethnocentrism binds us to our groups and communities. Yet these same mental processes can indeed get us into enormous trouble, as when stereotypes become blinders, distorting sight of the variation that occurs within any category, or when a cheerful affection for "us" produces a savage condemnation of "them."

Prisoners of Hate consists of three sections. Part I examines the cognitive distortions and beliefs that underlie the psychology of anger in everyday life. Part II examines violence in individuals and groups, from individuals who commit rape, assault, and child abuse to the collective illusions that legitimize prejudice and war. Part III considers the "brighter side of human nature"—the universal needs for attachment, altruism, and cooperation—and Beck's suggestions for the cognitive interventions that might reduce anger and violence between individuals, groups, or nations.

Beck, who is a skilled clinician and founder of his own Institute for Cognitive Therapy and Research in Philadelphia, is on strongest ground when he writes about anger and its resolution among individuals and couples. Cognitive therapy has a substantial and impressive track record of success in helping people resolve emotional problems such as depression, anxiety, panic, and anger. Indeed, hundreds of controlled studies have consistently found that cognitive therapy is more effective than "depth" or "talk" therapies such as psychoanalysis *and* more effective than medications such as antidepressants. The therapist teaches individuals to seek evidence for their beliefs; to consider alternate explanations of an annoying person's behavior; to solve problems rather than attack or withdraw and sulk; and to modify unrealistic or self-defeating expectations and beliefs. Beck has written numerous books for clinicians on the scientific grounding of cognitive therapy, and one popular book for bickering couples, *Love is Never Enough* (1988).

However, the methods that might work for an angry couple are unlikely to work on the grand scale that Beck envisions in *Prisoners of Hate*. Beck succumbs to the fallacy of the misleading similarity: If two phenomena share certain features, the phenomena must have the same causes and be modifiable by the same interventions.

Thus, having observed similar elements of primal thinking in individual and group behavior, Beck notes, "This is not surprising, since group behavior represents the cumulative effect of the individual members' thinking." This observation is plain wrong; group behavior is far more than the sum of its members' thoughts or even their individual wishes or personalities. Cognitive distortions and stereotypes about the enemy do indeed "activate the motivation to fight and kill," but, at a group level, so do many other forces, including conformity, group pressure, cultural values, loyalty to fellow soldiers, self-defense, fear, and direct orders.

As Beck himself observes, the same cognitive distortions that cause anger and hatred between individuals may be the results of conflict between groups. "Rather than hostile aggression causing wars," Beck acknowledges, "war causes hostile aggression." Many people believe that genocide, as in the horrifying examples of Rwanda and the former Yugoslavia, are a result of "age-old tribal hatreds." In fact, policies of genocide against a perceived enemy or scapegoat are almost always generated by governments that feel weakened and vulnerable.

Likewise, although there may indeed be commonalities of thought processes in all forms of anger and hatred, it does not follow that the same interventions are appropriate at individual and group levels. Beck believes that the interventions that work for warring couples are appropriate for warring groups and nations: deactivate hostility with a cooling-off period; encourage empathy; teach both sides that they might actually be abysmally wrong in their characterizations of one another's motives and intentions; and emphasize the satisfactions of cooperation and altruism.

How sane, how nice, how . . . unlikely! Cognitive therapy as a method, and Aaron Beck as a clinician, have a sweet optimism and rationality to them that are appealing, yet will strike many as naïve. "It is conceivable that if people were to question the validity of any of these [distorted, irrational] images or beliefs," he writes of people's thinking in wartime, "they might be less willing to kill other human beings." Well, yes, they might—if they also become less willing to be court-martialed for insubordination, imprisoned for being a conscientious objector, ostracized or even shot for being a traitor, or publicly humiliated for not joining in the fight against the enemy.

"Although the *causes* of conflicts are numerous and complex," Beck writes, "the *solutions* can be facilitated by greater attention to the psychology of leaders and followers on both sides." Were it only so easy. I can imagine how most leaders would respond to efforts to correct the "errors" in their thinking about their enemies. Likewise, efforts to change the "psychology of followers" so that people will magically decide to do the right thing—give women the vote, say, or abolish slavery—have had dismal success. It's hard enough to get someone you love to give up an entrenched attitude. Reducing prejudices on a larger scale requires long, hard, organized efforts to change laws and cultural practices.

Come, let us reason together, Beck exhorts us, and correct our mistaken beliefs about one another: "The 'voice of reason' is not necessarily quiet if we use appropriate methods to amplify it." Yet, as he himself amply documents, people *love* their irrational beliefs; *want* their cognitive distortions; and, most of all, *profit* from their biases and hatreds. Some profit psychologically, in inflated self-esteem and feeling that they belong to the best in-group; some profit socially, in having the support of their friends and colleagues; some profit financially. Politicians are quite aware of these benefits, which is why they hire ministers of propaganda and press secretaries to promote primal thinking on a national scale. Individuals and couples in conflict will benefit enormously from reading this book; but it will take more than reason to make governments reasonable.

74

16

■ ■ ■

Making Us Crazy
DSM: The Psychiatric Bible and the Creation of Mental Disorders

By Herb Kutchins and Stuart A. Kirk

America's most successful exports are violent movies, fast food, and diagnoses of mental illness, all of which can be dangerous to public health.

It is easy, looking backward, to see how diagnoses of mental illness reflected the biases of their time and supported the interests of those in power. In the American south before the Civil War, a physician named Samuel Cartwright argued that many slaves were suffering from two forms of mental illness: "drapetomania," whose primary symptom was the uncontrollable urge to escape from slavery, and "dysathesia aethiopica," whose symptoms were destroying property on the plantation, being disobedient, or refusing to work. Slaveowners were thereby reassured that a mental disorder, not the intolerable condition of slavery, made blacks seek freedom.

"Drapetomania" now sounds as dated as Plato's theory that female hysteria is caused by a lonely womb that wanders through the body crying for a baby. Surely, many people think, the bad old days of psychiatric misdiagnosis are past, thanks to modern technology and the scientific method. But as Herb Kutchins and Stuart A. Kirk show in *Making Us Crazy,* their superb analysis of the inherently subjective and political nature of labeling mental illness, drapetomania lives.

George Albee, a past president of the American Psychological Association, once observed that "Appendicitis, a brain tumor, and

Times Literary Supplement, October 29, 1999.

chicken pox are the same everywhere, regardless of culture or class; mental conditions, it seems, are not." Physicians do not take a vote to decide whether diabetes, cancer, and measles are physical illnesses; but psychiatrists still vote on what constitutes a mental illness. Is "Self-Defeating Personality Disorder" a mental illness? Yes or no? Are disobedient teenagers suffering from Oppositional Defiant Disorder or simply from Transitory Adolescent Insanity Behavior? Are you crazy if you want sex too often, or only if you don't want it enough? And how much sex is not enough?

The power to diagnose is power indeed, because the labels that people apply to their problems lead to different courses of action. If you think you are melancholy because your neurotransmitters are out of whack or because you have a gene for depression, you may be persuaded to take an antidepressant. If you think you are depressed because your job is in peril or because you are enmeshed in family battles, other solutions follow. Medical labels encourage us to look inward, to pathology in our genes, hormones, and brains; social and political explanations encourage us to look outward, to the conditions of our lives.

Making Us Crazy examines the forces that have contributed to the medicalizing of common human problems. Of these, undoubtedly the most influential is the *Diagnostic and Statistical Manual of Mental Disorders* (DSM), published by the American Psychiatric Association. The DSM is the bible of psychiatric diagnosis worldwide. In a brilliant orchestration of marketing and promotion, it has suc-

ceeded in transforming the normal difficulties of life into mental disorders and in fostering intrapsychic explanations of behavior that almost entirely overlook ethnicity, culture, class, gender, and circumstance.

Kutchins, a professor of social work, and Kirk, a professor of social welfare, reveal the shaky premises and biases inherent in the DSM's claims to scientific objectivity. The DSM has succeeded in standardizing the categories of who is, and who is not, mentally ill. Its categories and terminology have become the common language of most clinicians and researchers around the world. Virtually all major textbooks in psychiatry and psychology base their discussions of mental disorders on the DSM. And although the DSM cautions in a preface that its categories "may not be wholly relevant to legal judgments," its categories are often used in determining whether a defendant was fully responsible for committing a crime or was suffering diminished capacity as a result of some mental disorder.

The DSM strives to classify varieties of mental disorders and their symptoms with a degree of precision to a hundredth of a decimal point. Under Major Depressive Disorder, Recurrent, you will find:

296.36	In Full Remission
296.35	In Partial Remission
296.31	Mild
296.32	Moderate
296.33	Severe Without Psychotic Features
296.34	Severe With Psychotic Features
296.30	Unspecified

76

This seems impressive until you look closer. If the depression is in full remission, how do you know it's recurrent? How can you distinguish partial remission from mild or moderate depression? And what is "unspecified"? The purpose of such precise numbers, say the compilers of the DSM, is to enhance reliability (agreement in diagnosis) among clinicians.

However, as Kirk and Kutchins demonstrated in their previous book, *The Selling of DSM: The rhetoric of science in psychiatry,* the manual does not remotely meet this goal, for two reasons that go right to the heart of the dilemma of diagnosis. One is that human behavior is too complicated to be squeezed into neat pigeonholes; the second is that clinicians, being human, inevitably bring their own perceptions, biases, cultural norms, and vested interests to judging and labeling any behavior they observe. Given case studies for diagnosis, in which the individual's symptoms are described identically but the individual varies by gender or race, clinicians typically diagnose women as being more depressed than men, unemployed husbands as being more disturbed than traditional breadwinners, and black men as being more paranoid and severely disordered than anyone else. This in spite of all the DSM's precise numbers.

The effort to categorize and describe emotional and behavioral problems is not itself misguided; serious mental disorders, from crippling depression to the mental impairments of schizophrenia, occur in cultures everywhere, although they express themselves in differing cultural idioms. (In England and the United States, men tend not to express depression as women do, by crying, sleeping, eating, and talking; rather, men try to cope by working harder, drinking more, driving faster, or withdrawing into silence. In America, they may also go out and shoot a stranger.)

The problem, say Kutchins and Kirk, is the DSM's imperialistic tendency "to medicalize problems that are not medical, to find pathology where there is only pathos, and to pretend to understand phenomena by merely giving them a label and a code number." Thus, as the territory of psychiatry and clinical psychology has expanded, so has the DSM. The DSM-I, a 129-page spiral-bound pamphlet published in 1952, contained only a few basic categories of mental illness: brain disorders, mental deficiency, personality disorders, and "nondiagnostic terms for hospital record." The latter category included "dead on admission," probably the only diagnosis that psychiatrists have ever agreed on.

With each ensuing edition, the DSM grew fatter. The latest, DSM-IV, is 900 pages long and contains more than 300 disorders, which cover virtually anything a human being might do, from smoking too much to getting old. (The DSM-V is due out in 2013.) Under Learning Disorders, which clinicians are instructed to differentiate, somehow, from "normal variations in academic attainment and from scholastic difficulties due to lack of opportunity, poor teaching, or cultural factors," you will find:

315.0	Reading Disorder
315.1	Mathematics Disorder
315.2	Disorder of Written Expression

Caffeine Intoxication (305.90) may help with these problems, as long as you do not succumb to Caffeine-Induced Sleep Disorder (292.89).

Because the DSM has such powerful ramifications, Kutchins and Kirk argue that it is crucial to understand the "shabbiness of the scientific evidence" on which most mental disorders are created, and how, once created, those diagnoses become vulnerable to misuse. How did normal problems get included in a compendium of *mental disorders?* Where do old diagnoses go when they die, and where do new ones come from?

When the DSM's pretensions to science are blown away, argue Kutchins and Kirk, the basis for its diagnoses continues to be a vote of practitioners on the grounds of their clinical experience or insight: "We psychiatrists think this disorder belongs here, because we have seen it in our practice." Perhaps they have. Yet psychiatrists have seen many things that, over the years, have proved to be ephemera of the biases and beliefs of the time. They have seen drapetomania, hysteria, penis envy, nymphomania, multiple personality disorder, and "childhood masturbation disorder" (which at least was an improvement over all the cases of "masturbatory insanity" they observed in the late nineteenth century). As fads pass, they are voted out; current fads are voted in. Narcissistic Personality Disorder was eliminated in 1968 and restored in 1980; where did it go for 12 years?

Making Us Crazy shows how special-interest groups, cultural prejudices, and political pressures often determine whether a disorder gets into the DSM or is rejected. One of the chapters tells the story of homosexuality, which, correctly, was voted out of the DSM in 1973, in a decision that had far-reaching implications for gay rights. But the vote was not made on the basis of the research showing that gay people were no more mentally or emotionally disturbed than heterosexuals; it was made in response to pressure from gay activists, including gay psychiatrists, and from research-oriented psychiatrists who were trying to eliminate outdated psychoanalytic influences from the manual. The decision reflected a cultural change in beliefs about sexuality.

Kutchins and Kirk's second story follows the invention of Posttraumatic Stress Disorder (PTSD), which was added under pressure from Vietnam veterans who sought help in overcoming the aftereffects of war. "The price they paid," observe the authors, "was to be identified as mentally ill." Before long, PTSD mushroomed into a term applied to anyone who suffered a terrible experience, particularly female victims of rape and domestic violence. Of course people suffer from traumatic experiences, say Kutchins and Kirk, but their symptoms are *normal* responses, not signs of mental disorder.

Diagnostic labels would be fine, this book concludes, if they accurately defined a particular problem in a way that led to appropriate treatment, as diagnoses of disease often provide. The public may take small comfort, Kutchins and Kirk argue, from the belief that the "pain in their lives and communities can be explained by a psychiatric label and eradicated by a pill." But that, they believe, is a delusion for which the DSM has no label.

17

■■■

Of Two Minds

The Growing Disorder in American Psychiatry

By T. M. Luhrmann

It is as true of mental illness as William Goldman said of the movie business: No one knows anything. No one knows the causes of the delusions and bizarre behavior of schizophrenics, the roller-coaster cycle of manic depressives, the infuriating habits of borderline personalities, and the calculated cruelty of psychopaths. No one knows why medications help some people and have no effect on others. No one knows why psychotherapy helps some people and has no effect on others. And when medications or therapy do work, no one knows why they do.

But human beings can't stand not knowing; we are the explaining species. So we make up stories that work for a while, giving us the illusion of understanding: mental illness is caused by demons, by Satanic possession, by the build-up of pressure in the brain, by bad mothering (an eternally popular choice), by too much serotonin or too little. When the culture moves on and the story collapses, we find a new one. In the case of mental illness, the quest for the right story takes on a special urgency because of the anguish of sufferers and the high emotional and social cost to their families and communities.

Of Two Minds is the best book on mental illness and its treatment that I have read since Jonas Robitscher's *The Powers of Psychiatry* (1980), which foresaw the schisms and tensions in psychiatry that Tanya Luhrmann now illuminates so well. Robitscher, who was both a psychiatrist and a lawyer, wrote a societal-level view of the abuses of power wrought by arrogant practitioners whose diagnoses and treatments were no more scientific than phrenology or trepanning. If he

Times Literary Supplement, October 27, 2000.

79

gave us a bird's-eye view, Luhrmann gives us the view from the ground. An anthropologist by training and a psychoanalytically oriented scholar by kinship (her father is a psychiatrist), she takes her readers on an insider's tour of how psychiatrists come to see the world as they do. She is, she says, a "halfie" anthropologist, "someone who grew up half in the world she writes about professionally, like an anthropologist with an Egyptian father who goes off to live with the Bedouin."

Luhrmann went off to live with the psychiatrists. For four years, she took notes, tape-recorded conversations, attended classes for new psychiatrists, conducted therapy herself (informing patients that she was unlicensed), went to conferences, hung out in emergency rooms, psychoanalytic treatment centers, and biomedical research units, and seems to have read everything ever written on mental disorders. She observed people who were truly crazy—the man "found in his kitchen, holding his wife's bloody heart in his hands"—and others so crushed by anxiety or depression that their despair was contagious. What Luhrmann calls the "real story" of twentieth-century psychiatry is the real story of her book: "how complex mental illness is, how difficult it is to treat, and how, in the face of this complexity, people cling to coherent explanations like poor swimmers to a raft."

The two leading "coherent explanations" of, and treatments for, mental illness are the psychoanalytic model, which dominated the past century, and the biomedical, which will dominate this one. Although psychiatrists are supposed to prescribe medication where appropriate and also conduct psychotherapy, most do one or the other. The reason, Luhrmann shows, is that these approaches reflect profoundly different notions of what it means to be mentally ill. Are psychiatrists treating a disease or a person, trying to fix brain biochemistry or unconscious conflicts, relying on data or insight as their guide?

Those who espouse the biomedical model regard schizophrenia or depression as if these were disorders like heart disease or arthritis; the patient is considered a rational adult with a medical problem. If we do not know yet what causes schizophrenic delusions, the answer will be found in the brain or in the genes. In contrast, those who espouse a psychodynamic model, says Luhrmann, regard "distress as something much more complicated, something that involves the kind of person you are: your intentions, your loves and hates, your messy, complicated past. . . . From this vantage point, mental illness is in your mind and in your emotional reactions to other people." It is the mind that must be fixed, not the brain.

Luhrmann's intellect sides with biomedical advances, but her heart belongs to daddy—to psychodynamic theory. "If the moral authority of the scientist derives from the knowledge he acquires," she writes, "the moral authority of the analyst derives from the love he gives." I suspect this remark tells us more about her loving father than about analysts in general, who surely were not conveying much love to patients whom they were busily diagnosing with penis envy, mother loathing, or repressed rage at one thing or another (if they even spoke to the patient at all). "If the biomedical world takes responsibility for a patient's body," writes Luhrmann, "the psychodynamic one takes responsibility for a patient's soul and for teaching that person how to take responsibility for himself." That kind of pretty sentiment turns up in psychodynamic writings all the time, but she offers no evidence that many, let alone most, analysts have followed it in practice.

Overall, however, Luhrmann is scrupulously fair to both approaches. She shows how psychoanalysis was weakened by its failures to cure people, then brought to its knees by the cost-conscious health care revolution in America and by empirical research. A bacterium, *h. pylori*, causes ulcers, not "the introjected mother eating the stomach lining"; schizophrenia is not a result of having a "schizophrenogenic" mother. Luhrmann understands that interpretation and insight are unreliable sources of knowledge; that psychodynamic theories are unverifiable; and that analysts' insistence on clinging to unconscious processes as explanations of behavior blinded them to other explanations of their patients' suffering.

Yet biomedical approaches have their own limitations. In spite of the hype surrounding them, medications do not work for many patients. The dropout and relapse rate for people who take them is very high because the drugs often have unpleasant side effects (so psychiatrists prescribe other drugs to counteract them). Zealotry and blindness to alternative explanations are hardly limited to psychoanalysts; the history of biomedical interventions, from drugs to psychosurgery, is just as fraught with cruelty, ignorance, and error. Today, Luhrmann rightly fears, an exclusive reliance on the biomedical model overlooks the complicated individual rattling around in that brain, with all of that person's relationships, experiences, and perceptions. An older psychiatrist tells her, "So few of the residents have any interest in learning how to get close to a patient. . . I mourn at the passing of the torch to the biologists, however desirable it may be in some ways. I feel that something very special is going to be lost."

That is Luhrmann's message: Most people who are severely mentally ill need both medication *and* psychotherapy; but a cost-obsessed healthcare system is increasingly pressuring psychiatrists to prescribe a cocktail of medicines and let the patient go. What is lost is the healing power of human connection and care.

How do psychiatrists become indoctrinated into one or the other of the two therapeutic models? Luhrmann takes us into the daily education of new psychiatrists: the lectures they attend, their hospital routine, how they learn to diagnose and treat disorders. Perhaps the most alarming and revealing sentence describing their training is this: "No young psychiatrist is seriously expected to read much." There are no sanctions against residents who do not read assignments. Lectures are designed to offer practical skills, not information or intellectual substance. A lecturer will talk about what to do in therapy rather than why the therapy helps or what kind of therapy might be better. Residents get plenty of lectures on medication, but only to learn which ones to prescribe. Those who want to know why medications work (or fail to) or who take this information too seriously, a chief resident told Luhrmann, are the ones who will have trouble.

Psychiatrists learn their trade through apprenticeship and supervised practice; they are thrown into a maelstrom of psychiatric emergencies and expected to learn on their feet. New psychiatrists are expected to make diagnoses *fast*: in a minute, in 30 seconds. One student started out skeptical and uncomfortable about making such rapid diagnoses; but by the end of the year, says Luhrmann, "she saw the illnesses as clearly as when we suddenly catch on to an optical trick and can no longer see the feature that makes it a puzzle for everyone else. And with that she became confident."

Yet this confidence, which of course is the hallmark of socialization into any profession, can be hazardous when the profession is on shaky ground to begin with. And in psychiatry, diagnosis remains an inherently uncertain and subjective enterprise. That is why, clinicians continue to have notoriously unreliable agreement with one another. "One sees mood disorders where another sees personality disorders," Luhrmann observes. "One expert sees dissociative disorder where another sees histrionics." Yet everyone becomes confident that he or she is correct.

More worrisome, a profession based on apprenticeship rather than scholarship is one in which its members are generally expected to accept answers, not ask questions. Psychiatrists learn virtually nothing of what Luhrmann herself knows about the relevance of culture, history, and social psychology to their profession. They do not learn, for example, how culture affects people's experience of their symptoms, their recovery, their attitudes about seeking help. Psychiatrists do not learn how trends in the larger society affect the creation of diagnoses, and how, once in place, diagnoses increase the reporting and apparent frequency of the disorder. They learn little or nothing about iatrogenic disorders, those caused by psychiatrists themselves in pursuit of some fashionable syndrome.

Throughout her examination of modern psychiatry and its dilemmas, Luhrmann never turns her gaze from the painful moral themes of her story. Issues of morality and responsibility—on the part of psychiatrists, of society, and of the mentally ill themselves—permeate her discussion. How we conceptualize madness is a moral issue: "Madness is real, and it is an act of moral cowardice to treat it as a romantic freedom." How we think about culpability for our actions is a moral issue: "Biology is the great moral loophole of our age." How psychiatrists balance their obligations is a moral issue: What should you do about a suicidal patient whom you believe should be hospitalized, but whom the mental health system believes should be released? Keep the patient and incur a huge financial burden to the family? Let the patient go and risk causing a suicide?

Further, says Luhrmann, patients have moral responsibilities too. In the last chapter, she interviews a man with schizophrenia who speaks eloquently about what his symptoms mean, how he functions in spite of them, and how he teaches his mentally ill clients to take responsibility for their actions, even though these individuals have severe limitations in their functioning.

Finally, Luhrmann raises the moral issues involved in the way that we as a society conceive of mental illness and the priorities we place on helping those who suffer from it. "We are so tempted to see ourselves as fixable, perfectible brains," she writes, "but the loss of our souls is a high price to pay." If we understand mental illness as *only* biomedical, writes Luhrmann, "we deprive people of hope when their medication does not fully work. We deprive them of their sense of mastery over themselves, of full personhood in our world, of their ability to see themselves as thinking and feeling, just differently from other people. They become lesser persons, lesser agents, lesser moral beings. We deprive them of the commitment we feel toward full-fledged human beings." Towards the end of her book, Luhrmann quotes a psychiatrist who tells her wistfully that she is "seeing our profession in the beauty of its great sunset." Luhrmann has given us a magnificent painting of that sunset. We can predict that night must fall, but none of us can say what the next dawn will bring for psychiatry and for the mentally ill who so need help. The answer is our moral choice, and our responsibility.

PART IV

RESEARCH METHODS
AND SOCIAL ISSUES

18

■ ■ ■

The Hungry Gene
The Science of Fat
and the Future of Thin

By Ellen Ruppel Shell

A *New Yorker* cartoon says it all. It's a map of the United States with the following legend:

White areas = people who are too fat. Grey areas = people who are too thin.

The entire map is white, except for a tiny gray spot at Los Angeles.

In the last two decades, while psychologists, historians, and feminists were focused on understanding and treating the eating disorders of the too-thin (anorexia and bulimia), people all over the world have been getting fatter. Obesity now outranks tobacco as the number one threat to public health; it is a major risk factor in cardiovascular disease, early-onset diabetes, and many physical ailments.

This lively and superbly researched book by science writer Ellen Ruppel Shell begins with the alarming statistics: Half of the adult populations of England, Mexico, South America, Finland, Russia, Bulgaria, and Saudi Arabia are overweight or obese. Obesity rates are soaring in the Indian middle class, and even in China and Japan. At the same time, the weight-loss industry is making fortunes selling fraudulent, dangerous, or merely useless schemes, pills, diets, and contraptions to a public desperate to lose weight. You can get a shiny "Fat-Be-Gone" ring, said to produce the same effect as jogging six miles. I suppose it works, if you wear it while jogging.

The pharmaceutical industry is salivating. If they can develop a Fat-Be-Gone pill, they have an entire planet that needs it. As one researcher whom Shell interviewed said, "Obesity is the trillion-dollar disease."

Shell gives us the history of obesity and efforts to cure it, showing how the leading theories have changed over

Times Literary Supplement, March 21, 2003.

time: characterological (obesity is caused by gluttony, sloth, and a general "failure of will"), psychoanalytic (it's caused by an oral fixation, sexual maladjustment, emotional "hunger"), behavioral (overeating is just a bad habit), and today's leading contender, genetic and biological.

The evidence is now overwhelming that obesity has nothing to do with failed will power, unconscious dynamics, psychological problems, or bad habits. "Mother Nature wants her children to eat," writes Shell. Evolution designed our bodies to store fat in case of dire emergencies, such as famine or illness, and hence to make us crave foods that are fat and sweet. The trouble for modern human beings is that, mercifully, most of us don't encounter those dire emergencies any more. The body gains weight for a famine that never arrives.

To explore a case study of this worldwide phenomenon, Shell travels to Kosrae, a Micronesian island where most inhabitants are obese and rates of diabetes, hypertension, and heart disease are now as prevalent as coconuts. Kosraens no longer farm or fish; they are too busy with their office jobs. She visits every grocery store on the island, and finds "plenty of salty, sweet, and fatty imports." In Kosrae, as in the rest of the world, the genetic disposition to gain weight was not a problem when the only food available was fish and fruit. Enter polished white rice, cooking oil, fatty meats, and candy, and most adults on the island grew fat. "The very genes that once protected these South Sea Islanders and many other indigenous cultures from their punishing prehistory are today predisposing them to early death," writes Shell. "Rapid Westernization has rendered their highly efficient genes not protective, but lethal."

Shell takes readers through the fascinating world of obesity research, interviewing leading scientists such as the pioneers Albert Stunkard, who was the first to disprove the psychoanalytic belief in the "obese personality," and Stephen O'Rahilly, who identified a rare genetic defect in people whose obsession with food could not be quenched by eating even massive amounts. These scientists speak eloquently of how difficult it has been to promote an understanding of the biological mechanisms in weight gain and obesity in a world that still thinks fat people are, as O'Rahilly says, "nasty people whose disgusting behavior has made them so sick." Thin people claim the moral high ground, he tells Shell, but in fact they are just lucky.

The book is rather misleadingly called "the hungry gene," because there is, unfortunately, no single gene responsible for overweight. The links between eating and overweight are as complex as a crossword, as delicate as a snowflake. Dozens of genes and body chemicals are involved in appetite, metabolism rates, and weight regulation. There are receptors in the nose and mouth that keep urging us to eat more in the presence of appealing food, receptors in the gut telling us to quit, and chemicals signaling that we have stored enough fat or not enough. We are designed to eat more than we otherwise would when food is varied; when we don't have to expend much energy to get it; when we are in the company of good friends who are hearty eaters;

and when familial and cultural customs exert their pull. The complexity of these mechanisms explains why appetite suppressing drugs fail in the long run, and why a drug or intervention that affects one part of the eating–weight interaction might have an unintended influence on another.

Although Shell's book is primarily about how the predisposition toward obesity is "written in the genes," the last part examines the major non-genetic reasons for weight gain: lack of exercise; the prevalence of sweets and sweet drinks; inexpensive, high-fat, high-calorie meals; and oversized portions. The story of Big Food and its worldwide marketing tactics in creating these conditions is told even more forcefully in Eric Schlosser's *Fast Food Nation* and Greg Critser's *Fat Land*, but Shell does a splendid job too. For example, the Japanese used to regard sweets as being for children only. But this attitude is changing as Japan and other Asian cultures are being exposed to Western foods and sweet drinks and the advertising promoting them.

Big Food is so powerful in the era of globalization that controls may need to come from government as well as public opinion. People may learn about the dangers of smoking and decide, individually, to quit; but everyone needs to eat. And what if McDonald's is the only game in town? What if you're poor and can't afford a healthy diet, let alone find fruits and vegetables in your markets and restaurants? In one region of Finland that had serious obesity and heart disease problems, Shell reports, the government subsidized free salads and vegetables at restaurants. Vegetable consumption doubled, and cardiovascular disease dropped by 73 percent. The obesity epidemic, Shell concludes, "is less a matter of individual differences than of societal pressures, and of the power of the institutions that impose them. We can and should resist."

Agreed; but it will take organized protest and all our will power to do so.

19

■ ■ ■

The Genius Factory
Unravelling the Mysteries of the Nobel Prize Sperm Bank

By David Plotz

The Nobel Prize sperm bank was ill-conceived (so to speak), but it was the seminal influence on the generations of fertility institutes that followed it. Born in California in 1980, the Repository for Germinal Choice was the brainchild of Robert Graham, a 74-year-old optometrist who had made millions of dollars by inventing shatterproof plastic eyeglasses. Graham was one of those uniquely American characters—the self-made millionaire inventor who, assuming that success at making money imbues a man with wisdom on all matters of social importance, sets out boldly with an entrepreneurial but delusional scheme to improve mankind. I do mean mankind literally. Womankind is generally not very interesting to these guys.

Graham launched his bank with fanfare, announcing his intention to reverse the dumbing-down drift of evolution that was creating inferior humans; if genetic planning could improve animals and plants, he said, it could improve human beings. The right sperm could, anyway. Graham's plan proceeded on what sociologist Barbara Rothman has called the "woman as flowerpot" view of pregnancy: You put in a seed, and out pops the result nine months later. At first, Graham wanted only smart flowerpots—women who belonged to Mensa, for example—but he gave up that requirement right away. Moreover, Graham didn't value any old kind of intelligence; no Nobelists in literature, thank you, no winners of the Nobel Peace Prize, no cellists, no comedians. By intelligence, he meant

Times Literary Supplement, September 30, 2005.

90

one thing: having a practical, problem-solving ability—as David Plotz notes, "by miraculous coincidence, *exactly* the same kind of analytical talent he himself possessed."

At first, the Repository for Germinal Choice did not offer much choice. Graham had vials of sperm from several scientists, including three Nobel Prize winners, so the press immediately gave the Repository a new name: the Nobel Prize sperm bank. Over the next 19 years, only 215 children were born from the bank's donors and none to a Nobel winner. The bank closed in 1999, its founder dead, its records sealed. Nothing was known of the children, their mothers, or the donors. David Plotz, an editor at Slate.com, decided to investigate. Who were they? What happened to them? How, in only two decades, did the world change from one in which a sperm bank was exotic, disreputable, and shocking to one where potential parents shop for designer sperm as if they were choosing a pair of shoes? The Nobel Prize sperm bank died, Plotz writes, but all American sperm banks today are its heirs, although they don't like to acknowledge its influence. They all emphasize safety, the rigorous testing of donors, and "choice, choice, choice" in the attributes one seeks in a genetic father.

In this lively and touching book, Plotz travels between the historical and cultural story of sperm banks and the personal stories of donors and recipients. For a country supposedly so egalitarian and welcoming of diversity, America has always been fertile ground for eugenic theories and horrific applications of them, usually on the poor, the uneducated, the mentally ill, and of course women, usually without their consent and sometimes without their awareness. (The first case of "artificial impregnation" occurred in 1884, when a doctor injected a woman with sperm from a medical student, who had cheerfully volunteered, because her husband was infertile. The doctor had knocked the woman out with chloroform, and neither he nor her husband ever told her the truth of how she happened to conceive.) By the time Graham opened the Repository, people were no longer interested in improving the race, just in improving their children. Old-time eugenics is dead, Plotz writes, but "private eugenics has arrived to replace it. If we can get better genes for our own kids, many of us will do so. Just like the first Nobel sperm bank customers, we are captive to the great delusion that we can control our children, that we can make them what we want them to be, rather than what they are."

However, Graham had a problem: Few Nobel Prize winners liked his idea, let alone were willing to donate their sperm, and the scientists who *were* willing to donate wanted to be anonymous. Riding to the rescue came William Shockley, who had won a Nobel for his invention of the transistor and who shared Graham's vision of improving the race genetically. Shockley acknowledged publicly that he was a donor, thereby giving the "Nobel Prize sperm bank" its name and credibility. Unfortunately for Graham, though, Shockley wouldn't shut up. He aroused public outrage by spewing his racist eugenic beliefs to all who would listen, humiliating his family in the process. Thus, he told *Playboy* that he was disappointed with his own children, who were "a very significant regression" from his own abilities; but after all, he added, their mother lacked his own academic achievements. Shockley, Plotz writes, turned the sperm bank "from a curiosity into a menace and then into a joke." People began making fun of the whole enterprise. How about a specialty sperm bank for Academy Award winners? For writers?

In spite of Shockley, in spite of the jokes, and in spite of the non-Nobel and non-noble sperm in the Repository, the bank began to thrive. A woman named Afton Blake conceived a baby she called Doron (Greek and Hebrew for "gift"), whose abilities she promoted like a press agent on speed. Doron was an infant prodigy and media darling, and within two years of his birth and attendant publicity, more than one thousand women had submitted applications to the sperm bank. So Graham and his staff set out to recruit more donors, relaxing the requirement of genius. They quickly learned that American women didn't much care about having sperm from smart men; they wanted sperm from men who were handsome, tall, and athletic.

Plotz soon found himself acting as detective and matchmaker, tracking down donors and brokering meetings with their offspring. These stories are the moral and emotional heart of the book. "Donor White" fathered 19 children, but became deeply attached to the one whose mother sought him out. His reaction is the reason that sperm banks forbid such meetings; donor offspring become real children who laugh, play, have personalities, give you trouble, and make you proud. In this case, the father needed the daughter more than she needed him; she was a contented child who had no emotional void to fill.

Other children had a hole in their souls, and longed to find a "real" father unlike their distant stepdads, or to have any father at all. Many were disappointed. One young man, expecting to find a loving, genius dad, got Jeremy—"an obscure doctor," Plotz writes, "whose notable accomplishment in life was leaving a wake of ex-wives and forgotten children." Plotz also interviewed the faintly creepy son of a Nobelist who became a donor—the son, not the dad. The son made a career of donating sperm because, he said, "the *main* game of the universe, the *only* game that matters, is the game of evolution, and you win by passing on genes. And I wanted to *win!*" Here, said Plotz, is just what Graham hoped to produce, "yet all I saw in him was the fickleness of DNA: Here was a Nobel Prize baby, and he was no prize at all."

That's the point, of course. As we are learning in this era of behavioral genetics, genes contribute far more than we once believed to personality, temperament, abilities, and diseases; yet they are not the sole ingredients in the recipe for a human being, nor can they ever be. In 1921, Lewis Terman began following more than 1,500 children with IQ scores in the top 1 percent of the population. (William Shockley did not make the cut when Terman was recruiting; his IQ of 129 was too low, Plotz tells us, "a slight that Shockley carried with him to the grave.") The children started out bright, healthy, and well adjusted. In adulthood, most became successful in the traditional ways of the times: men in careers and women as homemakers. Yet some of the most gifted men failed to live up to their early promise, dropping out of school and ending up doing low-level work. Parental encouragement and the child's own motivation, not IQ, made the difference between those who did well and those who drifted aimlessly through life.

And Doron Blake, the genius child, the prodigy? At the time Plotz interviewed him, he was planning to teach high school. He was as articulate and smart as Graham could have hoped for, yet he rejected all that Graham preached about genetics and intelligence. "Genes have never been important to me," he told Plotz. "Family is the people you love. I feel a lot closer to people who are not my blood than to those that are."

If Robert Graham had opened a food bank for the poor instead of a sperm bank for the rich, he could have made a real difference in human IQ; after World War II, IQs have steadily risen in most countries all over the world, largely a result of better nutrition for children and pregnant women. Or perhaps, given the consistent level of human stupidity that produces war, terrorism, greed, and folly, Graham should have stuck with inventing things; plastic eyeglasses were an indisputable contribution to the improvement of the species.

Graham died in 1997, at a meeting of the American Association for the Advancement of Science, where he had gone to recruit sperm donors. He fell in the hotel bathtub and drowned. Plotz, with his unerring eye for detail and irony, noted that *Time* magazine marked Graham's death in its Milestones column, just above the news that the biologist Carleton Gajdusek, a Nobel Prize winner, had been convicted of child molestation.

20

■ ■ ■

Rape

A History From 1860 to the Present

By Joanna Bourke

Andrew Luster, the wealthy great-grandson of cosmetics magnate Max Factor, was convicted of raping three women after drugging them with a powerful sedative. He was convicted on 20 counts of rape, 17 counts of raping an unconscious victim and multiple counts of sodomy and oral copulation. He was sentenced to 124 years in prison and will be eligible for parole in 100 years.

Worlds away from the wealth and privilege of Andrew Luster, Private Lynndie England, along with other female and male American soldiers, inflicted sexual, physical, and psychological abuse on Iraqi prisoners of war. The photo of this 22-year-old working-class woman, smirking as she held a naked prisoner on a leash, stunned and enraged observers around the world. Private England was sentenced to three years in a military prison and was paroled after serving 521 days.

Halfway through Joanna Bourke's travels through the psychological and social history of rape, she notices that "The most startling conclusion is that the community of sexually violent individuals is extremely heterogeneous." Some rape for the psychosexual thrill and will do it as often as they can, there being no treatment for their sadistic desires; others commit sexual assault under the abnormal conditions of war and will never do it again once they are home; others rape in packs or gangs, largely as display to other males or to humiliate and conquer their victims; and many rape out of narcissistic self-delusion, persuading themselves that their victim really "wanted it" or that they, the rapists, were "entitled." Rapists have different sexual preferences, they don't share

Times Literary Supplement, February 1, 2008.

personality traits, and they have different degrees of empathy toward their victims. Some have mental disorders and others have none; some resort to violence and others rely on manipulation and charm. Some rapists are women.

The trajectory from Susan Brownmiller's *Against Our Will*, published in 1975—with its impassioned, stinging call to arms, "rape is a conscious process of intimidation by which *all* men keep *all* women in a state of fear"—to Joanna Bourke's *Rape: A history from 1860 to the present* reveals how much our understanding of rape has changed in thirty years and how little we still know. Brownmiller's generation of feminists made it impossible to regard rape ever again as a subject of jokes, justifications ("you can't rape an unwilling woman"), and psychoanalytic nonsense ("all women want to be raped"). They raised public awareness of the prevalence and emotional consequences of rape, by lovers as well as strangers, and, as Bourke documents, their efforts changed British and American law and the prosecution of rape cases. Husbands may no longer rape their wives—their "property"—as part of their conjugal rights. Date rape became a legal reality. Men may press charges against rapists of either sex. (Bourke cites studies suggesting that between 3 and 16 per cent of men have experienced forced sex, and that between 6 and 24 per cent of the perpetrators were women.) Parts of the body deemed legally violable have expanded; oral and anal penetration are now part of the definition, along with penetration of any orifice by objects other than the penis. Rules of evidence have been reformed: Judges no longer issue a warning to jurors about the need for corroboration nor caution jurors that the complainant might be lying. Limits have been placed upon the cross-examination of the victim, to minimize the "second rape" that victims often felt in the courtroom.

Bourke wrote this book, she tells us, when she "became enraged" upon learning that "only 5 per cent of rapes reported to the police in the UK even end in a conviction" today, compared to 33 percent in the 1970s. These are surprising numbers indeed, and Bourke takes them to mean that "men are still getting away with rape, despite three decades of rigorous feminist lobbying and extensive law reform." The primary reason for the low conviction rate, she argues, is the persistence, among jurists and the general public, of "rape myths"— that women lie, that pressuring a reluctant or ambivalent woman is not rape, that a woman's "no" does not really mean no, and that it is the woman's responsibility, not the man's, to control the man's sexual behavior.

But perhaps the conviction rate was higher in the 1970s precisely because women were much less likely to report rape in those days: thus, those who were willing to go to trial and subject themselves to further harassment might have had a more convincing case. As Bourke herself notes, between 1985 and 2003, rapes reported to the police in Britain increased from 1,842 to 12,293. Perhaps, again because of "feminist lobbying and extensive law reform," that increase includes kinds of rape allegations that are more difficult to prosecute—more dependent on he said/she said testimony and less on evidence of physical brutality.

Bourke's book begins and ends with the problem of conviction rates. In between she examines how the "rapist" (a word first used in 1883) has been conceptualized, explained, and treated in England and America since 1860. Apparently Bourke chose that start date because she believes that the "sexualization of rape is a modern phenomenon": nineteenth-century working women did not experience rape as a sexual attack or a harm to the self but rather as an attack on their social standing and class position; rapists did not use the language of sexual gratification (theirs or their victims') until the twentieth century. Because Bourke does not consider rape in other cultures, nonwestern religions, or history before the mid-nineteenth century, it is difficult to assess this argument.

Nonetheless, her selection of topics—including chapters on theories, therapies, female perpetrators, exhibitionists, sexual psychopaths, and rape in three "violent institutions" (the home, prisons, and the military)—reveals the complexity of the problem and its intransigence. As Bourke shows, the contemporary notion that rape is an "evolutionary adaptation" cannot account for homosexual rape, gang rape, rape that does not involve vaginal penetration, rape of girls and women past menopause, and the interesting fact that many rapists do not ejaculate. Social explanations of rape (violent subcultures, poverty, bad homes) and psychoanalytic theories (castrating mothers, neurotic or sexually immature personalities) do no better in predicting who becomes a sexual predator or a date-rape opportunist. Nor has anyone developed a successful therapy for most chronic offenders, though many interventions have been tried, including extreme procedures such as castration, sterilization, lobotomy, and behavioral counter-conditioning programs. Bourke cites one behavioral therapist who said, "It is no easy task to induce a person to give up what to him is exquisite pleasure."

Bourke is prepared to acknowledge that rates of female violence, including acts of rape and sexual coercion, are rising, and that it is not antifeminist to admit it: "Arguing that 'women do it too' need not be part of a feminist backlash," Bourke writes, "but an engagement within feminism about the nature of sexual violence." I wish she had been bold enough to carry this attitude throughout her book. It is indisputable that too many women have been, and still are, disbelieved when they claim they have been raped. But is the solution to believe all claims made by women? How, in the absence of videotapes (which convicted Luster and England) or evidence of physical brutality, can even the most sympathetic jurors determine culpability? How does society meet the challenge of bringing justice to rape victims without increasing the risk of convicting innocent defendants? (In America, the Innocence Project has, using DNA testing, exonerated more than 100 men who had been wrongly imprisoned on rape charges.) "We also need to take the protection of civil liberties [for the accused] seriously," Bourke notes; I should hope so.

Likewise, it is time for feminists to speak frankly about false allegations and not leave this touchy subject to misogynists and self-justifying rapists. Bourke regards the possibility that some women make false charges as one of the persistent myths that let rapists go free; she repeats an old, unvalidated statistic that only two per cent do. But Eugene Kanin, who has been studying male sexual violence for decades, found that by the 1980s the rate of false allegation had risen to nearly half of reported rapes in a university setting and also in a police department in a small town in the American midwest. In the latter study, Kanin investigated every single rape allegation made to the police from 1978 to 1987, and found that 41 per cent were eventually declared false by the complainant herself. The women said that they had lied for one of three all-too-human reasons: providing an alibi for infidelity, getting revenge, and wanting attention or sympathy.

The bitter problem for feminists to confront, then, is that one possible result of feminist activism—making women more comfortable filing charges against their rapists—may have produced an increase in false allegations as well. Bourke says that in the US, "complaints by African-American women are often simply dismissed by the police"—which indeed they were, in 1966, when the study she cites was done. Is that still true today? Some jurisdictions, especially college campuses, may now be hyper-responsive to complaints made by black women. Certainly Michael Nifong, the disbarred prosecutor in North Carolina, believed the black female stripper who falsely accused four male Duke University lacrosse players.

Bourke's history of rape's definitions and treatments contains much of interest, but its central failing is that rather than offer a nuanced investigation into sexual relations today, the author envelops the subject in postmodern fog. Rape, by definition, is unwanted sex, but not all unwanted sex is rape, and Bourke's book would have been a far greater contribution if she had clarified the difference. Instead, she muddies it: "I have adopted much broader definitions of rape and sexual abuse than those established by law," Bourke writes, "on the grounds that judicial definitions fail to encompass the full range of sexual acts that have been constituted as abusive (nonconsensual or forced) over time." She argues that for an act to be called "sexual abuse" two components must be present: a person has to identify the act as sexual, "however they may wish to define the term 'sexual'. Second, the individual must also claim that the act was nonconsensual, *unwanted* or coerced, *however they may wish to define those terms*" (my emphasis).

This postmodern way of defining the problem—it is whatever you think it is, and whenever you decide it is—would, if taken seriously, absolve women of any responsibility for their sexual decisions, exacerbate sexual misunderstandings, and create a nightmare for the law. "Judges, jurors and law-enforcement officers still have no idea where the boundary between 'bad sex' and rape lies," Bourke notes, and readers of this book will have the same difficulty. Should a man be sent to prison for bad sex or for pressing a woman to have sex with him by buying her gifts and dinners?

Moreover, in recent research, many women report having had unwanted intercourse that they in no way construed as rape; some did so for the negative reasons that Bourke condemns as abuse (the partner made them feel guilty or obligated) but others for positive reasons (they wanted to satisfy their curiosity or please their partners). Bourke doesn't get to have it both ways: It's rape if she thinks it is, but it's also rape if the victim doesn't think it is. The goal indeed is to make it possible for all women (and men) to safely say no, and to this, I would add another: to not fear the repercussions or regrets of having said yes.

21

■ ■ ■

Sex and the Psyche

By Brett Kahr

Of all scholarly endeavors, studying sex is the hardest. (The second hardest is writing about sex.) Not only do people frequently lie to the interviewer; they also lie to themselves. Even when people try to be honest with themselves, they usually have little or no idea why they do what they do, or why one thing turns them on and not another. And even when they try to be honest with the interviewer, they often misremember, distorting their memories to accord with their current self-perceptions. Thus, studies of people who are followed over time find that men and women remember having had fewer sexual partners than they really did, they remember having far more sex with those partners than they actually had, they remember being more sexually adventurous as teenagers than they actually were, and they remember using condoms more often than they actually did.

In addition to the wobbly reliability of answers, there is the vexed matter of questions, because what you ask, and of whom, constrains what you learn. Sexologists once hotly debated whether women's rape fantasies were evidence of women's allegedly natural masochism or passivity; they rarely questioned men about their fantasies of being raped, assuming that men, the dirty curs, would fantasize only from the standpoint of the rapist. When researchers began asking both sexes the same questions, as I did for an admittedly unrepresentative magazine survey years ago, no differences emerged between women and men in the likelihood of fantasizing about being raped. Of course, given that it was a fantasy, "rape" generally meant being tied up and forced to endure deliciously arousing sexual activities with incredibly exciting perpetrators.

Anyone willing to leap into the prickly thicket of sex research, therefore, is to be commended for the desire, although in this domain as in so many others, desire alone is not enough. Technique is essential. Brett Kahr is a Freudian psychotherapist, most at home doing therapy. For this project, he

Times Literary Supplement, May 11, 2007.

hired the polling company YouGov to conduct a random-sample computer survey, which produced a respectable rate of return from several thousand Britons; interviewed people for "background color" for the television documentary that is sponsoring some of the research; conducted clinical interviews, in which he unfortunately administered those psychodynamically popular but scientifically unreliable projective tests like the Rorschach; and solicited written fantasies from the research project's website.

The resulting 600-page tome is an amalgam of clinical case studies; answers to the survey questions, including tables of percentages of the frequency of various sexual activities (including masturbation, extramarital sex, and activities from fondling to anal sex); and a generous sampling of the 19,000 fantasies Kahr accumulated, which apparently did not bore him rigid. These range from terse sentence fragments ("sex with my sister-in-law") to long graphic paragraphs ("When I jerk off, which is a lot—two or three times a day, 365 days a year—I wank to thoughts of my uncle . . . ," followed by the details, and I do mean the details).

Yet somehow, in spite of the author's undeniably cheerful exertions, the results will leave many readers unsatisfied. You will learn that people's private sexual fantasies are sources of both pleasure and misery. There is no such thing as a normal sexual fantasy. We don't know why people have them, except that fantasies produce arousal, and arousal, evolutionarily speaking, is a good thing. Fantasies serve "a multiplicity of interrelated

functions." Everyone has them. Millions of people have fantasies that, if carried out, would land them in jail. You should share your fantasies with your partner, except when you shouldn't. You should be careful about sharing them with your friends, because if the friendship ends, your favorite fantasy involving your sister-in-law might come back to haunt you. Trying to act out your fantasy will most likely be a dud, except sometimes it will be kind of fun. Your fantasies are mostly not dangerous, except when they are. If your fantasies are boring, it does not necessarily mean that you are, and if they are outlandish, it does not necessarily mean you are crazy. And so on.

In any study, the answers you get are only as good as the questions you ask. Kahr's questions are framed by his psychoanalytic training and assumptions, for example, that current sexual feelings and conscious fantasies must have their origins in the experiences and unconscious fantasies of early childhood and infancy, indeed earlier than that. Unfortunately, he, like most analysts, holds the outdated view that memories of abuses that occur in the first few years of life, the time of infantile amnesia, can be accessed "in the course of a lengthy period of psychotherapy or psychoanalysis." Modern research finds, however, that infantile amnesia reflects normal cognitive and biological immaturity, not the repression of trauma.

Thus, Kahr says, "he particularly wanted to know whether a correlation could be established between early histories of abuse and later fantasies of abusing others or of being abused oneself." This is a reasonable question, albeit a narrow one, as it overlooks the more powerful, proximal impact upon fantasy of advertising, income, exposure to erotica and pornography, social class, adult experiences with violence, feelings of powerlessness, and cultural norms. But even granted Kahr's interest in early abuse, his inexperience in survey research and its analysis is reflected in the two questions he asks to ascertain its effects:

- "At any point in your lifetime, have you ever been subject to any kind of physical, sexual or emotional abuse? Please be as honest as possible and include anything that you have experienced, whether or not you have told anybody or reported it."
- "Please tell us at what age you were first subjected to this form of abuse."

How could anyone answer a multiple-choice question that conflates physical, sexual, and emotional abuse, without defining any of these terms? What if your parents spanked you rarely but severely, and you did not think it was abuse at the time because every child you knew was also hit? What if your first serious lover routinely humiliated and belittled you? What if an older relative or minister fondled you once when you were seven? How can Kahr know which experience—the single act of molesta-tion, the rare but severe beatings, or the continual humiliation in your first adult affair—your answer reflects? How can you be expected to remember when your parents first spanked you?

Kahr justifies the blurring of terms in this question as a problem of not having space in the questionnaire; but if space is a problem, the solution is not to combine questions but to narrow them, to be clear about what the answers might signify. His questions on unwanted sex—"Has anybody ever forced or convinced you to have sex when you actually did not want to?" and the age at which this occurred—are better, though combining "forced" and "convinced" does muddy the issue.

Those who read *Sex and the Psyche* for its empirical findings may be interested in the statistics on who is doing what and with which and to whom and how often. It may be reassuring to know that most people are not having sex more often than you are, or doing more exciting things than you are. Other readers may prefer Kahr's vivid case studies, although if they are reading the book for these sexy stories I suspect they are likely to be disappointed. The cumulative effect of the pages and pages of stories of licking, biting, sucking, masturbating, peeing, and preening is oddly antisexual—proving once again that fantasies, like children, are most interesting to the people who have them.